SUSE OpenStack Cloud 6 - Admin User Guide

A catalogue record for this book is available from the Hong Kong Public Libraries.

Published in Hong Kong by Samurai Media Limited.

Email: info@samuraimedia.org

ISBN 978-988-8406-46-3

Contents

1 Documentation Conventions

The following notices and typographical conventions are used in this documentation:

Warning

Vital information you must be aware of before proceeding. Warns you about security issues, potential loss of data, damage to hardware, or physical hazards.

Important

Important information you should be aware of before proceeding.

Note

Additional information, for example about differences in software versions.

Tip

Helpful information, like a guideline or a piece of practical advice.

```
tux > command
```

Commands than can be run by any user, including the root user.

```
root # command
```

Commands that must be run with root privileges. In many cases you can also prefix these commands with the **sudo** command to run them.

2 How can I administer an OpenStack cloud?

As an OpenStack cloud administrative user, you can manage tenants, known as projects, users, services, images, flavors, and quotas.

The examples in this guide show you how to perform tasks by using the following methods:

- OpenStack dashboard. Use this web-based graphical interface, code named horizon (https://git.openstack.org/cgit/openstack/horizon) ↗, to view, create, and manage resources and services.

- OpenStack command-line clients. Each core OpenStack project has a command-line client that you can use to run simple commands to view, create, and manage resources and services in a cloud and automate tasks by using scripts.

You can modify these examples for your specific use cases.

In addition to these ways of interacting with a cloud, you can access the OpenStack APIs directly or indirectly through cURL (http://curl.haxx.se) ↗ commands or open SDKs. You can automate access or build tools to manage resources and services by using the native OpenStack APIs or the EC2 compatibility API.

To use the OpenStack APIs, it helps to be familiar with HTTP/1.1, RESTful web services, the OpenStack services, and JSON or XML data serialization formats.

2.1 Who should read this book?

This book is written for administrators who maintain and secure an OpenStack cloud installation to serve end users' needs. You should have years of experience with Linux-based tools for system administration. You should also be familiar with OpenStack basics, such as managing projects and users, troubleshooting, performing backup and recovery, and monitoring. For more information, see the OpenStack Operations Guide (http://docs.openstack.org/ops) ↗.

3 OpenStack dashboard

As a cloud administrative user, the OpenStack dashboard lets you create and manage projects, users, images, and flavors. You can also set quotas, and create and manage services. For information about using the dashboard to perform end user tasks, see the OpenStack End User Guide (http://docs.openstack.org/user-guide/) ↗.

3.1 Log in to the dashboard

The dashboard is generally installed on the controller node.

1. Ask the cloud operator for the host name or public IP address from which you can access the dashboard, and for your user name and password.

2. Open a web browser that has JavaScript and cookies enabled.

    Note

   To use the Virtual Network Computing (VNC) client for the dashboard, your browser must support HTML5 Canvas and HTML5 WebSockets. The VNC client is based on noVNC. For details, see noVNC: HTML5 VNC Client (https://github.com/kanaka/noVNC/blob/master/README.md) ↗. For a list of supported browsers, see Browser support (https://github.com/kanaka/noVNC/wiki/Browser-support) ↗.

3. In the address bar, enter the host name or IP address for the dashboard, for example `https://ipAddressOrHostName/`.

    Note

   If a certificate warning appears when you try to access the URL for the first time, a self-signed certificate is in use, which is not considered trustworthy by default. Verify the certificate or add an exception in the browser to bypass the warning.

4. On the Log In page, enter your user name and password, and click *Sign In*.
   The top of the window displays your user name. You can also access the *Settings* tab (*Section 3.1.4, "OpenStack dashboard — Settings tab"*) or sign out of the dashboard.

The visible tabs and functions in the dashboard depend on the access permissions, or roles, of the user you are logged in as.

- If you are logged in as an end user, the *Project* tab (*Section 3.1.1, "OpenStack dashboard — Project tab"*) and *Identity* tab (*Section 3.1.3, "OpenStack dashboard — Identity tab"*) are displayed.

- If you are logged in as an administrator, the *Project* tab (*Section 3.1.1, "OpenStack dashboard — Project tab"*) and *Admin* tab (*Section 3.1.2, "OpenStack dashboard — Admin tab"*) and *Identity* tab (*Section 3.1.3, "OpenStack dashboard — Identity tab"*) are displayed.

3.1.1 OpenStack dashboard — *Project* tab

Projects are organizational units in the cloud, and are also known as tenants or accounts. Each user is a member of one or more projects. Within a project, a user creates and manages instances.

From the *Project* tab, you can view and manage the resources in a selected project, including instances and images. You can select the project from the drop down menu at the top left.

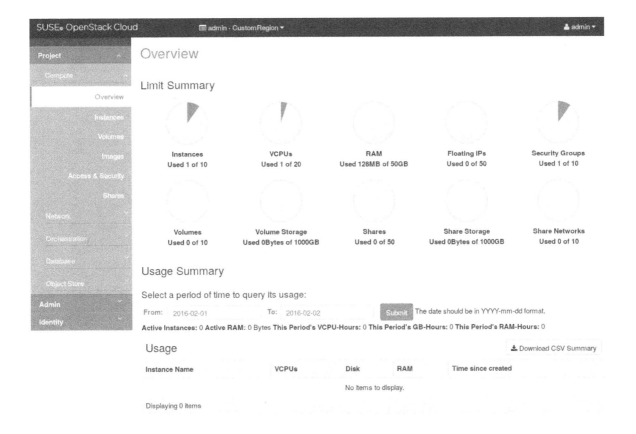

FIGURE 3.1: PROJECT TAB

From the *Project* tab, you can access the following categories:

3.1.1.1 *Compute* tab

- *Overview*: View reports for the project.

- *Instances*: View, launch, create a snapshot from, stop, pause, or reboot instances, or connect to them through VNC.

- *Volumes*: Use the following tabs to complete these tasks:

  - *Volumes*: View, create, edit, and delete volumes.

  - *Volume Snapshots*: View, create, edit, and delete volume snapshots.

- *Images*: View images and instance snapshots created by project users, plus any images that are publicly available. Create, edit, and delete images, and launch instances from images and snapshots.

- *Access & Security*: Use the following tabs to complete these tasks:

  - *Security Groups*: View, create, edit, and delete security groups and security group rules.

  - *Key Pairs*: View, create, edit, import, and delete key pairs.

  - *Floating IPs*: Allocate an IP address to or release it from a project.

  - *API Access*: View API endpoints.

3.1.1.2 *Network* tab

- *Network Topology*: View the network topology.

- *Networks*: Create and manage public and private networks.

- *Routers*: Create and manage routers.

3.1.1.3 *Orchestration* tab

- *Stacks*: Use the REST API to orchestrate multiple composite cloud applications.

- *Resource Types*: Show a list of all the supported resource types for HOT templates.

3.1.1.4 *Object Store* tab

- *Containers*: Create and manage containers and objects.

3.1.2 OpenStack dashboard — *Admin* tab

Administrative users can use the *Admin* tab to view usage and to manage instances, volumes, flavors, images, networks and so on.

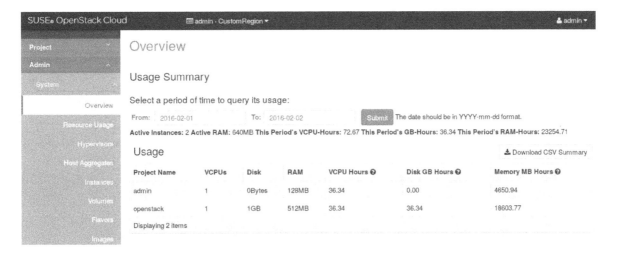

FIGURE 3.2: ADMIN TAB

From the *Admin* tab, you can access the following category to complete these tasks:

3.1.2.1 *System* tab

- *Overview*: View basic reports.

- *Resource Usage*: Use the following tabs to view the following usages:

    - *Usage Report*: View the usage report.

    - *Stats*: View the statistics of all resources.

- *Hypervisors*: View the hypervisor summary.

- *Host Aggregates*: View, create, and edit host aggregates. View the list of availability zones.

- *Instances*: View, pause, resume, suspend, migrate, soft or hard reboot, and delete running instances that belong to users of some, but not all, projects. Also, view the log for an instance or access an instance through VNC.

- *Volumes*: Use the following tabs to complete these tasks:

    - *Volumes*: View, create, manage, and delete volumes.

    - *Volume Types*: View, create, manage, and delete volume types.

    - *Volume Snapshots*: View, manage, and delete volume snapshots.

- *Flavors*: View, create, edit, view extra specifications for, and delete flavors. A flavor is size of an instance.

- *Images*: View, create, edit properties for, and delete custom images.

- *Networks*: View, create, edit properties for, and delete networks.

- *Routers*: View, create, edit properties for, and delete routers.

- *Defaults*: View default quota values. Quotas are hard-coded in OpenStack Compute and define the maximum allowable size and number of resources.

- *Metadata Definitions*: Import namespace and view the metadata information.

- *System Information*: Use the following tabs to view the service information:

    - *Services*: View a list of the services.

    - *Compute Services*: View a list of all Compute services.

    - *Block Storage Services*: View a list of all Block Storage services.

    - *Network Agents*: View the network agents.

    - *Orchestration Services*: View a list of all Orchestration services.

3.1.3   OpenStack dashboard — *Identity* tab

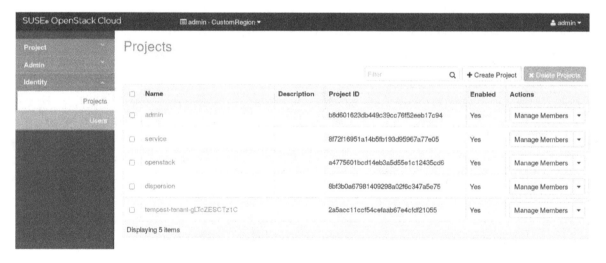

FIGURE 3.3: IDENTITY TAB

- *Projects*: View, create, assign users to, remove users from, and delete projects.

- *Users*: View, create, enable, disable, and delete users.

3.1.4   OpenStack dashboard — *Settings* tab

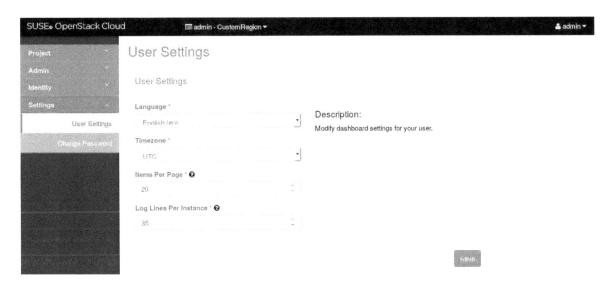

FIGURE 3.4: SETTINGS TAB

Click the *Settings* button from the user drop down menu at the top right of any page, you will see the *Settings* tab.

- *User Settings*: View and manage dashboard settings.

- *Change Password*: Change the password of the user.

3.2   Create and manage images

As an administrative user, you can create and manage images for the projects to which you belong. You can also create and manage images for users in all projects to which you have access.

To create and manage images in specified projects as an end user, see the OpenStack End User Guide (http://docs.openstack.org/user-guide/) ↗.

To create and manage images as an administrator for other users, use the following procedures.

3.2.1 Create images

For details about image creation, see the Virtual Machine Image Guide (http://docs.openstack.org/image-guide/) ↗.

1. Log in to the dashboard.
   Choose the *admin* project from the drop-down list at the top of the page.

2. On the *Admin* tab, open the *System* tab and click the *Images* category. The images that you can administer for cloud users appear on this page.

3. Click *Create Image,* which opens the *Create An Image* window.

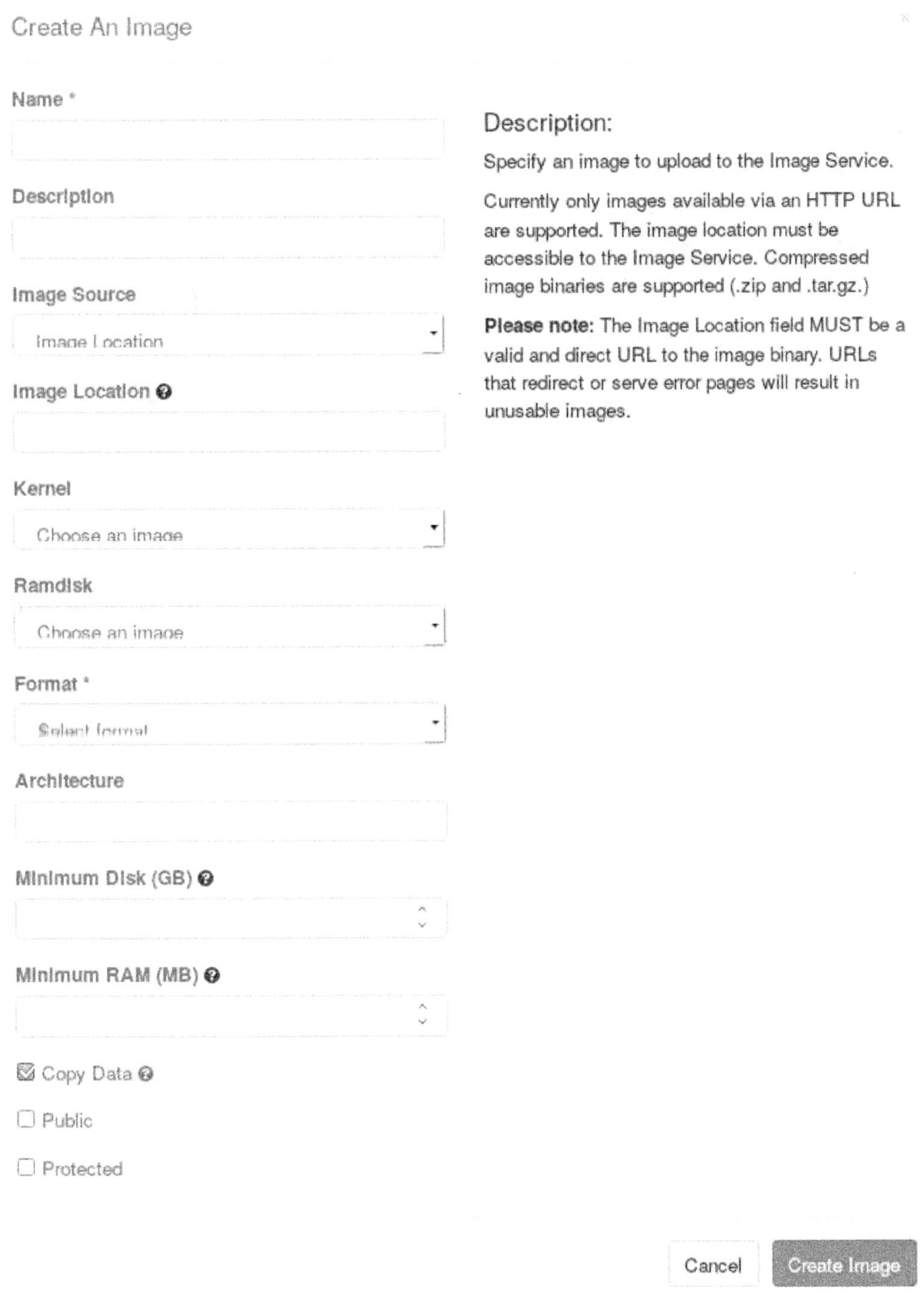

Create An Image

Name *

[   ]

Description

[   ]

Image Source

[Image Location   ▾]

Image Location ❓

[   ]

Kernel

[Choose an image   ▾]

Ramdisk

[Choose an image   ▾]

Format *

[Select format   ▾]

Architecture

[   ]

Minimum Disk (GB) ❓

[⌃⌄]

Minimum RAM (MB) ❓

[⌃⌄]

☑ Copy Data ❓

☐ Public

☐ Protected

Description:

Specify an image to upload to the Image Service.

Currently only images available via an HTTP URL are supported. The image location must be accessible to the Image Service. Compressed image binaries are supported (.zip and .tar.gz.)

Please note: The Image Location field MUST be a valid and direct URL to the image binary. URLs that redirect or serve error pages will result in unusable images.

[Cancel] [Create Image]

FIGURE 3.5: DASHBOARD — CREATE IMAGE

4. In the *Create An Image* window, enter or select the following values:

Name	Enter a name for the image.
Description	Enter a brief description of the image.
Image Source	Choose the image source from the drop-down list. Your choices are *Image Location* and *Image File*.
Image File or Image Location	Based on your selection, there is an *Image File* or *Image Location* field. You can include the location URL or browse for the image file on your file system and add it.
Kernel	Select the kernel to boot an AMI-style image.
Ramdisk	Select the ramdisk to boot an AMI-style image.
Format	Select the image format.
Architecture	Specify the architecture. For example, `i386` for a 32-bit architecture or `x86_64` for a 64-bit architecture.
Minimum Disk (GB)	Leave this field empty.
Minimum RAM (MB)	Leave this field empty.
Copy Data	Specify this option to copy image data to the Image service.
Public	Select this option to make the image public to all users.
Protected	Select this option to ensure that only users with permissions can delete it.

5. Click *Create Image*.

   The image is queued to be uploaded. It might take several minutes before the status changes from `Queued` to `Active`.

3.2.2 Update images

1. Log in to the Dashboard. Choose the *admin* project from the drop-down list at the top of the page.

2. On the *Admin* tab, open the *System* tab and click the *Images* category.

3. Select the images that you want to edit. Click *Edit Image*.

4. In the *Update Image* window, you can change the image name.
   Select the *Public* check box to make the image public. Clear this check box to make the image private. You cannot change the *Kernel ID*, *Ramdisk ID*, or *Architecture* attributes for an image.

5. Click *Update Image*.

3.2.3 Delete images

1. Log in to the Dashboard. Choose the *admin* project from the drop-down list at the top of the page.

2. On the *Admin tab*, open the *System* tab and click the *Images* category.

3. Select the images that you want to delete.

4. Click *Delete Images*.

5. In the *Confirm Delete Images* window, click *Delete Images* to confirm the deletion.
   You cannot undo this action.

3.3 Create and manage roles

A role is a personality that a user assumes to perform a specific set of operations. A role includes a set of rights and privileges. A user assumes that role inherits those rights and privileges.

Note

OpenStack Identity service defines a user's role on a project, but it is completely up to the individual service to define what that role means. This is referred to as the service's policy. To get details about what the privileges for each role are, refer to the `policy.json` file available for each service in the `/etc/SERVICE/policy.json` file. For example, the policy defined for OpenStack Identity service is defined in the `/etc/keystone/policy.json` file.

3.3.1 Create a role

1. Log in to the dashboard and choose the *admin* project from the *CURRENT PROJECT* drop-down list.

2. On the *Admin* tab, click the *Roles* category.

3. Click the *Create Role* button.
   In the *Create Role* window, enter a name for the role.

4. Click the *Create Role* button to confirm your changes.

3.3.2 Edit a role

1. Log in to the dashboard and choose the *admin* project from the *CURRENT PROJECT* drop-down list.

2. On the *Admin* tab, click the *Roles* category.

3. Click the *Edit* button.
   In the *Update Role* window, enter a new name for the role.

4. Click the *Update Role* button to confirm your changes.

 Note

Using the dashboard, you can edit only the name assigned to a role.

3.3.3 Delete a role

1. Log in to the dashboard and choose the *admin* project from the *CURRENT PROJECT* drop-down list.

2. On the *Admin* tab, click the *Roles* category.

3. Select the role you want to delete and click the *Delete Roles* button.

4. In the *Confirm Delete Roles* window, click *Delete Roles* to confirm the deletion. You cannot undo this action.

3.4 Manage instances

As an administrative user, you can manage instances for users in various projects. You can view, terminate, edit, perform a soft or hard reboot, create a snapshot from, and migrate instances. You can also view the logs for instances or launch a VNC console for an instance.

For information about using the Dashboard to launch instances as an end user, see the OpenStack End User Guide (http://docs.openstack.org/user-guide/dashboard_launch_instances.html) ↗ .

3.4.1 Create instance snapshots

1. Log in to the Dashboard and choose the *admin* project from the drop-down list at the top of the page.

2. On the *Admin* tab, open the *System* tab and click the *Instances* category.

3. Select an instance to create a snapshot from it. From the *Actions* drop-down list, select *Create Snapshot.*

4. In the *Create Snapshot* window, enter a name for the snapshot.

5. Click *Create Snapshot.* The Dashboard shows the instance snapshot in the *Images* category.

6. To launch an instance from the snapshot, select the snapshot and click *Launch Instance.* For information about launching instances, see the OpenStack End User Guide (http:// docs.openstack.org/user-guide/dashboard_launch_instances.html) ↗ .

3.4.2 Control the state of an instance

1. Log in to the Dashboard and choose the *admin* project from the drop-down list at the top of the page.

2. On the *Admin* tab, open the *System* tab and click the *Instances* category.

3. Select the instance for which you want to change the state.

4. From the drop-down list in the *Actions* column, select the state.
   Depending on the current state of the instance, you can perform various actions on the instance. For example, pause, un-pause, suspend, resume, soft or hard reboot, or terminate (actions in red are dangerous).

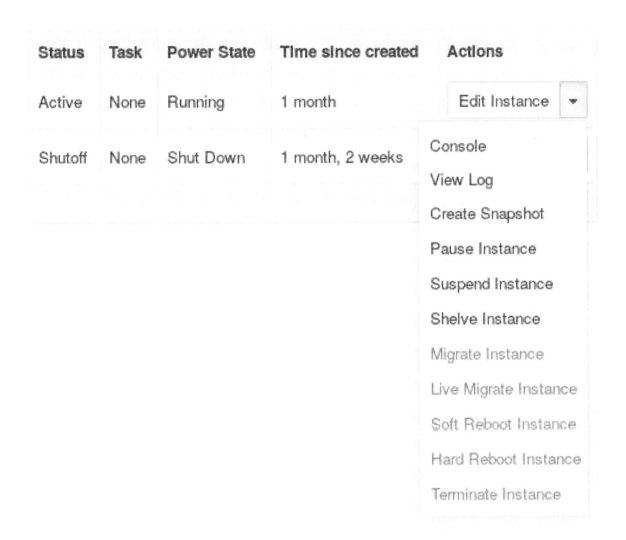

Status	Task	Power State	Time since created	Actions
Active	None	Running	1 month	Edit Instance ▾
Shutoff	None	Shut Down	1 month, 2 weeks	

Console
View Log
Create Snapshot
Pause Instance
Suspend Instance
Shelve Instance
Migrate Instance
Live Migrate Instance
Soft Reboot Instance
Hard Reboot Instance
Terminate Instance

FIGURE 3.6: FIGURE DASHBOARD — INSTANCE ACTIONS

3.4.3 Track usage

Use the *Overview* category to track usage of instances for each project.

You can track costs per month by showing meters like number of VCPUs, disks, RAM, and uptime of all your instances.

1. Log in to the Dashboard and choose the *admin* project from the drop-down list at the top of the page.

2. On the *Admin* tab, open the *System* tab and click the *Overview* category.

3. Select a month and click *Submit* to query the instance usage for that month.

4. Click *Download CSV Summary* to download a CSV summary.

3.5 Manage flavors

In OpenStack, a flavor defines the compute, memory, and storage capacity of a virtual server, also known as an instance. As an administrative user, you can create, edit, and delete flavors. The following table lists the default flavors.

Flavor	VCPUs	Disk (in GB)	RAM (in MB)
m1.tiny	1	1	512
m1.small	1	20	2048
m1.medium	2	40	4096
m1.large	4	80	8192
m1.xlarge	8	160	16384

3.5.1 Create flavors

1. Log in to the dashboard.
   Choose the *admin* project from the drop-down list at the top of the page.

2. In the *Admin* tab, open the *System* tab and click the *Flavors* category.

3. Click *Create Flavor*.

4. In the *Create Flavor* window, enter or select the parameters for the flavor in the *Flavor Information* tab.

Name	Enter the flavor name.
ID	Unique ID (integer or UUID) for the new flavor. If specifying 'auto', a UUID will be automatically generated.
VCPUs	Enter the number of virtual CPUs to use.
RAM (MB)	Enter the amount of RAM to use, in megabytes.
Root Disk (GB)	Enter the amount of disk space in gigabytes to use for the root (/) partition.
Ephemeral Disk (GB)	Enter the amount of disk space in gigabytes to use for the ephemeral partition. If unspecified, the value is 0 by default. Ephemeral disks offer machine local disk storage linked to the lifecycle of a VM instance. When a VM is terminated, all data on the ephemeral disk is lost. Ephemeral disks are not included in any snapshots.
Swap Disk (MB)	Enter the amount of swap space (in megabytes) to use. If unspecified, the default is 0.

5. In the *Flavor Access* tab, you can control access to the flavor by moving projects from the *All Projects* column to the *Selected Projects* column.

   Only projects in the *Selected Projects* column can use the flavor. If there are no projects in the right column, all projects can use the flavor.

6. Click *Create Flavor*.

3.5.2   Update flavors

1. Log in to the dashboard.

2. Choose the *admin* project from the drop-down list at the top of the page.

3. In the *Admin* tab, open the *System* tab and click the *Flavors* category.

4. Select the flavor that you want to edit. Click *Edit Flavor*.

5. In the *Edit Flavor* window, you can change the flavor name, VCPUs, RAM, root disk, ephemeral disk, and swap disk values.

6. Click *Save*.

3.5.3 Update Metadata

1. Log in to the dashboard.
   Choose the *admin* project from the drop-down list at the top of the page.

2. In the *Admin* tab, open the *System* tab and click the *Flavors* category.

3. Select the flavor that you want to update. In the drop-down list, click *Update Metadata* or click *No* or *Yes* in the *Metadata* column.

4. In the *Update Flavor Metadata* window, you can customize some metadata keys, then add it to this flavor and set them values.

5. Click *Save*.
   Optional metadata keys

TABLE 3.1: OPTIONAL METADATA KEYS

CPU limits	quota:cpu_shares
quota:cpu_period	
quota:cpu_limit	
quota:cpu_reservation	
quota:cpu_quota	
Disk tuning	quota:disk_read_bytes_sec
quota:disk_read_iops_sec	
quota:disk_write_bytes_sec	

quota:disk_write_iops_sec	
quota:disk_total_bytes_sec	
quota:disk_total_iops_sec	
Bandwidth I/O	quota:vif_inbound_average
quota:vif_inbound_burst	
quota:vif_inbound_peak	
quota:vif_outbound_average	
quota:vif_outbound_burst	
quota:vif_outbound_peak	
Watchdog behavior	hw:watchdog_action
Random-number generator	hw_rng:allowed
hw_rng:rate_bytes	
hw_rng:rate_period	

For information about supporting metadata keys, see the OpenStack Cloud Administrator Guide (http://docs.openstack.org/admin-guide-cloud/compute-flavors.html) ↗.

3.5.4   Delete flavors

1. Log in to the dashboard.

2. Choose the *admin* project from the drop-down list at the top of the page.

3. In the *Admin* tab, open the *System* tab and click the *Flavors* category.

4. Select the flavors that you want to delete.

5. Click *Delete Flavors*.

6. In the *Confirm Delete Flavors* window, click *Delete Flavors* to confirm the deletion. You cannot undo this action.

3.6   Manage volumes and volume types

Volumes are the Block Storage devices that you attach to instances to enable persistent storage. Users can attach a volume to a running instance or detach a volume and attach it to another instance at any time. For information about using the dashboard to create and manage volumes as an end user, see the OpenStack End User Guide (http://docs.openstack.org/user-guide/dashboard_manage_volumes.html) ↗.

As an administrative user, you can manage volumes and volume types for users in various projects. You can create and delete volume types, and you can view and delete volumes. Note that a volume can be encrypted by using the steps outlined below.

3.6.1   Create a volume type

1. Log in to the dashboard and choose the *admin* project from the drop-down list at the top of the page.

2. On the *Admin* tab, open the *System* tab and click the *Volumes* category.

3. Click the *Volume Types* tab, and click *Create Volume Type* button. In the *Create Volume Type* window, enter a name for the volume type.

4. Click *Create Volume Type* button to confirm your changes.

 Note

A message indicates whether the action succeeded.

3.6.2   Create an encrypted volume type

1. Create a volume type using the steps above for *Section 3.6.1, "Create a volume type"*.

2. Click *Create Encryption* in the Actions column of the newly created volume type.

3. Configure the encrypted volume by setting the parameters below from available options (see table):

Provider

Specifies the class responsible for configuring the encryption.

Control Location

Specifies whether the encryption is from the front end (nova) or the back end (cinder).

Cipher

Specifies the encryption algorithm.

Key Size (bits)

Specifies the encryption key size.

4. Click *Create Volume Type Encryption.*

Encryption Options

The table below provides a few alternatives available for creating encrypted volumes.

Encryption parameters	Parameter options	Comments
Provider	nova.volume.encryptors. luks.LuksEncryptor (Recommended)	Allows easier import and migration of imported encrypted volumes, and allows access key to be changed without re-encrypting the volume
nova.volume.encryptors. cryptsetup. CryptsetupEncryptor	Less disk overhead than LUKS	
Control Location	front-end (Recommended)	The encryption occurs within nova so that the data transmitted over the network is encrypted
back-end	This could be selected if a cinder plug-in supporting an encrypted back-end block	

Encryption parameters	Parameter options	Comments
	storage device becomes available in the future. TLS or other network encryption would also be needed to protect data as it traverses the network	
Cipher	aes-xts-plain64 (Recommended)	See NIST reference below to see advantages*
aes-cbc-essiv	Note: On the command line, type 'cryptsetup benchmark' for additional options	
Key Size (bits)	512 (Recommended for aes-xts-plain64. 256 should be used for aes-cbc-essiv)	Using this selection for aes-xts, the underlying key size would only be 256-bits*
256	Using this selection for aes-xts, the underlying key size would only be 128-bits*	

* **Source** NIST SP 800-38E (http://csrc.nist.gov/publications/nistpubs/800-38E/nist-sp-800-38E.pdf) ↗

3.6.3 Delete volume types

When you delete a volume type, volumes of that type are not deleted.

1. Log in to the dashboard and choose the *admin* project from the drop-down list at the top of the page.

2. On the *Admin* tab, open the *System* tab and click the *Volumes* category.

3. Click the *Volume Types* tab, select the volume type or types that you want to delete.

4. Click *Delete Volume Types* button.

5. In the *Confirm Delete Volume Types* window, click the *Delete Volume Types* button to confirm the action.

 Note

A message indicates whether the action succeeded.

3.6.4 Delete volumes

When you delete an instance, the data of its attached volumes is not destroyed.

1. Log in to the dashboard and choose the *admin* project from the drop-down list at the top of the page.

2. On the *Admin* tab, open the *System* tab and click the *Volumes* category.

3. Select the volume or volumes that you want to delete.

4. Click *Delete Volumes* button.

5. In the *Confirm Delete Volumes* window, click the *Delete Volumes* button to confirm the action.

 Note

A message indicates whether the action succeeded.

3.7 Manage shares and share types

Shares are file storage that instances can have access to. Users can allow or deny a running instance to have access to a share at any time. For information about using the dashboard to create and manage shares as an end user, see the OpenStack End User Guide (http://docs.openstack.org/user-guide/dashboard_manage_shares.html) ↗.

As an administrative user, you can manage shares and share types for users in various projects. You can create and delete share types, and you can view and delete shares.

3.7.1 Create a share type

1. Log in to the dashboard and choose the *admin* project from the drop-down list at the top of the page.

2. On the *Admin* tab, open the *System* tab and click the *Shares* category.

3. Click the *Share Types* tab, and click *Create Share Type* button. In the *Create Share Type* window, enter or select the following values.
   Name: Enter a name for the share type.
   Driver handles share servers: Choose True or False
   Extra specs: To add extra specs, use key = value.

4. Click *Create Share Type* button to confirm your changes.

 Note

A message indicates whether the action succeeded.

3.7.2 Update share type

1. Log in to the dashboard and choose the *admin* project from the drop-down list at the top of the page.

2. On the *Admin* tab, open the *System* tab and click the *Shares* category.

3. Click the *Share Types* tab, select the share type that you want to update.

4. Select *Update Share Type* from Actions.

5. In the *Update Share Type* window, update extra specs.
   Extra specs: To add extra specs, use key = value. To unset extra specs, use key.

6. Click *Update Share Type* button to confirm your changes.

 Note

A message indicates whether the action succeeded.

3.7.3 Delete share types

When you delete a share type, shares of that type are not deleted.

1. Log in to the dashboard and choose the *admin* project from the drop-down list at the top of the page.

2. On the *Admin* tab, open the *System* tab and click the *Shares* category.

3. Click the *Share Types* tab, select the share type or types that you want to delete.

4. Click *Delete Share Types* button.

5. In the *Confirm Delete Share Types* window, click the *Delete Share Types* button to confirm the action.

 Note

A message indicates whether the action succeeded.

3.7.4 Delete shares

1. Log in to the dashboard and choose the *admin* project from the drop-down list at the top of the page.

2. On the *Admin* tab, open the *System* tab and click the *Shares* category.

3. Select the share or shares that you want to delete.

4. Click *Delete Shares* button.

5. In the *Confirm Delete Shares* window, click the *Delete Shares* button to confirm the action.

 Note

A message indicates whether the action succeeded.

3.7.5 Delete share server

1. Log in to the dashboard and choose the *admin* project from the drop-down list at the top of the page.

2. On the *Admin* tab, open the *System* tab and click the *Share Servers* category.

3. Select the share that you want to delete.

4. Click *Delete Share Server* button.

5. In the *Confirm Delete Share Server* window, click the *Delete Share Server* button to confirm the action.

 Note

A message indicates whether the action succeeded.

3.7.6 Delete share networks

1. Log in to the dashboard and choose the *admin* project from the drop-down list at the top of the page.

2. On the *Admin* tab, open the *System* tab and click the *Share Networks* category.

3. Select the share network or share networks that you want to delete.

4. Click *Delete Share Networks* button.

5. In the *Confirm Delete Share Networks* window, click the *Delete Share Networks* button to confirm the action.

 Note

A message indicates whether the action succeeded.

3.8 View and manage quotas

To prevent system capacities from being exhausted without notification, you can set up quotas. Quotas are operational limits. For example, the number of gigabytes allowed for each tenant can be controlled so that cloud resources are optimized. Quotas can be enforced at both the tenant (or project) and the tenant-user level.

Typically, you change quotas when a project needs more than ten volumes or 1 TB on a compute node.

Using the Dashboard, you can view default Compute and Block Storage quotas for new tenants, as well as update quotas for existing tenants.

 Note

> Using the command-line interface, you can manage quotas for the OpenStack Compute service, the OpenStack Block Storage service, and the OpenStack Networking service (see). Additionally, you can update Compute service quotas for tenant users.

The following table describes the Compute and Block Storage service quotas:

Quota Descriptions

TABLE 3.2: QUOTA DESCRIPTIONS

Quota Name	Defines the number of	Service
Gigabytes	Volume gigabytes allowed for each project.	Block Storage
Instances	Instances allowed for each project.	Compute
Injected Files	Injected files allowed for each project.	Compute
Injected File Content Bytes	Content bytes allowed for each injected file.	Compute
Keypairs	Number of keypairs.	Compute
Metadata Items	Metadata items allowed for each instance.	Compute
RAM (MB)	RAM megabytes allowed for each instance.	Compute

Quota Name	Defines the number of	Service
Security Groups	Security groups allowed for each project.	Compute
Security Group Rules	Rules allowed for each security group.	Compute
Snapshots	Volume snapshots allowed for each project.	Block Storage
VCPUs	Instance cores allowed for each project.	Compute
Volumes	Volumes allowed for each project.	Block Storage

3.8.1   View default project quotas

1. Log in to the OpenStack dashboard.

2. On the *Admin* tab, open the *System* tab and click the *Defaults* category.

3. The default quota values are displayed.

 Note

You can sort the table by clicking on either the *Quota Name* or *Limit* column headers.

3.8.2   Update project quotas

1. Log in to the OpenStack dashboard.

2. On the *Admin* tab, open the *System* tab and click the *Defaults* category.

3. Click the *Update Defaults* button.

4. In the *Update Default Quotas* window, you can edit the default quota values.

5. Click the *Update Defaults* button.

Note

The dashboard does not show all possible project quotas. To view and update the quotas for a service, use its command-line client. See .

3.9 View cloud resources

3.9.1 View services information

As an administrative user, you can view information for OpenStack services.

1. Log in to the OpenStack dashboard and choose the *admin* project from the drop-down list at the top of the page.

2. On the *Admin* tab, click the *System Information* category.
   View the following information on these tabs:

   - *Services*: Displays the internal name and the public OpenStack name for each service, the host on which the service runs, and whether or not the service is enabled.

   - *Compute Services*: Displays information specific to the Compute service. Both host and zone are listed for each service, as well as its activation status.

   - *Block Storage Services*: Displays information specific to the Block Storage service. Both host and zone are listed for each service, as well as its activation status.

   - *Network Agents*: Displays the network agents active within the cluster, such as L3 and DHCP agents, and the status of each agent.

   - *Orchestration Services*: Displays information specific to the Orchestration service. Name, engine id, host and topic are listed for each service, as well as its activation status.

3.9.2 View cloud usage statistics

The Telemetry service provides user-level usage data for OpenStack-based clouds, which can be used for customer billing, system monitoring, or alerts. Data can be collected by notifications sent by existing OpenStack components (for example, usage events emitted from Compute) or by polling the infrastructure (for example, libvirt).

 Note

You can only view metering statistics on the dashboard (available only to administrators). The Telemetry service must be set up and administered through the `ceilometer` command-line interface (CLI).

For basic administration information, refer to the "Measure Cloud Resources" chapter in the OpenStack End User Guide (http://docs.openstack.org/user-guide/) ↗.

3.9.2.1 View resource statistics

1. Log in to the OpenStack dashboard as a user with Admin privileges.

2. On the *Admin* tab, click the *Resource Usage* category.

3. Click the:

   - *Usage Report* tab to view a usage report per tenant (project) by specifying the time period (or even use a calendar to define a date range).

   - *Stats* tab to view a multi-series line chart with user-defined meters. You group by project, define the value type (min, max, avg, or sum), and specify the time period (or even use a calendar to define a date range).

3.10 Create and manage host aggregates

Host aggregates enable administrative users to assign key-value pairs to groups of machines.

Each node can have multiple aggregates and each aggregate can have multiple key-value pairs. You can assign the same key-value pair to multiple aggregates.

The scheduler uses this information to make scheduling decisions. For information, see Scheduling (http://docs.openstack.org/liberty/config-reference/content/section_compute-
scheduler.html) ↗.

3.10.1   To create a host aggregate

1. Log in to the dashboard.
   Choose the *admin* project from the drop-down list at the top of the page.

2. On the *Admin* tab, open the *System* tab and click the *Host Aggregates* category.

3. Click *Create Host Aggregate.*

4. In the *Create Host Aggregate* dialog box, enter or select the following values on the *Host Aggregate Information* tab:

   * *Name*: The host aggregate name.

   * *Availability Zone*: The cloud provider defines the default availability zone, such as `us-west`, `apac-south`, or `nova`. You can target the host aggregate, as follows:

     * When the host aggregate is exposed as an availability zone, select the availability zone when you launch an instance.

     * When the host aggregate is not exposed as an availability zone, select a flavor and its extra specs to target the host aggregate.

5. Assign hosts to the aggregate using the *Manage Hosts within Aggregate* tab in the same dialog box.
   To assign a host to the aggregate, click + for the host. The host moves from the *All available hosts* list to the *Selected hosts* list.

You can add one host to one or more aggregates. To add a host to an existing aggregate, edit the aggregate.

3.10.2   To manage host aggregates

1. Choose the *admin* project from the drop-down list at the top of the page.

2. On the *Admin* tab, open the *System* tab and click the *Host Aggregates* category.

- To edit host aggregates, select the host aggregate that you want to edit. Click *Edit Host Aggregate.*
  In the *Edit Host Aggregate* dialog box, you can change the name and availability zone for the aggregate.

- To manage hosts, locate the host aggregate that you want to edit in the table. Click *More* and select *Manage Hosts.*
  In the *Add/Remove Hosts to Aggregate* dialog box, click + to assign a host to an aggregate. Click - to remove a host that is assigned to an aggregate.

- To delete host aggregates, locate the host aggregate that you want to edit in the table. Click *More* and select *Delete Host Aggregate.*

3.11 Launch and manage stacks using the Dashboard

The Orchestration service provides a template-based orchestration engine for the OpenStack cloud. Orchestration services create and manage cloud infrastructure resources such as storage, networking, instances, and applications as a repeatable running environment.

Administrators use templates to create stacks, which are collections of resources. For example, a stack might include instances, floating IPs, volumes, security groups, or users. The Orchestration service offers access to all OpenStack core services via a single modular template, with additional orchestration capabilities such as auto-scaling and basic high availability.

For information about:

- administrative tasks on the command-line, see .

 Note

There are no administration-specific tasks that can be done through the Dashboard.

- the basic creation and deletion of Orchestration stacks, refer to the OpenStack End User Guide (http://docs.openstack.org/user-guide/dashboard_stacks.html) ↗ .

4 OpenStack command-line clients

4.1 Overview

Each OpenStack project provides a command-line client, which enables you to access the project API through easy-to-use commands. For example, the Compute service provides a nova command-line client.

You can run the commands from the command line, or include the commands within scripts to automate tasks. If you provide OpenStack credentials, such as your user name and password, you can run these commands on any computer.

Internally, each command uses cURL command-line tools, which embed API requests. OpenStack APIs are RESTful APIs, and use the HTTP protocol. They include methods, URIs, media types, and response codes.

OpenStack APIs are open-source Python clients, and can run on Linux or Mac OS X systems. On some client commands, you can specify a debug parameter to show the underlying API request for the command. This is a good way to become familiar with the OpenStack API calls.

As a cloud end user, you can use the OpenStack dashboard to provision your own resources within the limits set by administrators. You can modify the examples provided in this section to create other types and sizes of server instances.

The following table lists the command-line client for each OpenStack service with its package name and description.

OpenStack services and clients

TABLE 4.1: OPENSTACK SERVICES AND CLIENTS

Service	Client	Package	Description
Application catalog	murano	python-muranoclient	Creates and manages applications.
Block Storage	cinder	python-cinderclient	Creates and manages volumes.
Clustering service	senlin	python-senlinclient	Creates and manages clustering services.

Service	Client	Package	Description
Compute	nova	python-novaclient	Creates and manages images, instances, and flavors.
Containers service	magnum	python-magnumclient	Creates and manages containers.
Database service	trove	python-troveclient	Creates and manages databases.
Data processing	sahara	python-saharaclient	Creates and manages Hadoop clusters on OpenStack.
Deployment service	fuel	python-fuelclient	Plans deployments.
Identity	keystone	python-keystoneclient	Creates and manages users, tenants, roles, endpoints, and credentials.
Image service	glance	python-glanceclient	Creates and manages images.
Key Manager service	barbican	python-barbicanclient	Creates and manages keys.
Monitoring	monasca	python-monascaclient	Monitoring solution.
Networking	neutron	python-neutronclient	Configures networks for guest servers.
Object Storage	swift	python-swiftclient	Gathers statistics, lists items, updates metadata, and uploads, downloads, and deletes files stored by the Object Storage service. Gains

Service	Client	Package	Description
			access to an Object Storage installation for ad hoc processing.
Orchestration	heat	python-heatclient	Launches stacks from templates, views details of running stacks including events and resources, and updates and deletes stacks.
Rating service	cloudkitty	python-cloudkittyclient	Rating service.
Shared file systems	manila	python-manilaclient	Creates and manages shared file systems.
Telemetry	ceilometer	python-ceilometerclient	Creates and collects measurements across OpenStack.
Telemetry v3	gnocchi	python-gnocchiclient	Creates and collects measurements across OpenStack.
Workflow service	mistral	python-mistralclient	Workflow service for OpenStack cloud.
Common client	openstack	python-openstackclient	Common client for the OpenStack project.

4.2   Install the OpenStack command-line clients

Install the prerequisite software and the Python package for each OpenStack client.

4.2.1   Install the prerequisite software

Most Linux distributions include packaged versions of the command-line clients that you can install directly, see *Section 4.2.2.2, "Installing from packages"*.

If you need to install the source package for the command-line package, the following table lists the software needed to run the command-line clients, and provides installation instructions as needed.

Prerequisite	Description
Python 2.7 or later	Currently, the clients do not support Python 3.
setuptools package	Installed by default on Mac OS X.
	Many Linux distributions provide packages to make setuptools easy to install. Search your package manager for setuptools to find an installation package. If you cannot find one, download the setuptools package directly from https://pypi.python.org/pypi/setuptools ↗.
	The recommended way to install setuptools on Microsoft Windows is to follow the documentation provided on the setuptools website (https://pypi.python.org/pypi/setuptools ↗). Another option is to use the unofficial binary installer maintained by Christoph Gohlke (http://www.lfd.uci.edu/~gohlke/pythonlibs/#setuptools (http://www.lfd.uci.edu/~gohlke/pythonlibs/#setuptools) ↗).
pip package	To install the clients on a Linux, Mac OS X, or Microsoft Windows system, use pip. It is easy to use, ensures that you get the latest version of the clients from the Python Package Index (https://pypi.python.org/) ↗, and lets you update or remove the packages later on.
	Since the installation process compiles source files, this requires the related Python development package for your operating system and distribution.
	Install pip through the package manager for your system:
	MacOS
	``
	# easy_install pip
	``
	Microsoft Windows

Prerequisite	Description
	Ensure that the `C:\Python27\Scripts` directory is defined in the `PATH` environment variable, and use the `easy_install` command from the setuptools package:

```
C:\>easy_install pip
```

Another option is to use the unofficial binary installer provided by Christoph Gohlke (http://www.lfd.uci.edu/~gohlke/python-libs/#pip ↗).

Ubuntu and Debian

```
# apt-get install python-dev python-pip
```

Note that extra dependencies may be required, per operating system, depending on the package being installed, such as is the case with Tempest.

Red Hat Enterprise Linux, CentOS, or Fedora.

A packaged version enables you to use yum to install the package:

```
# yum install python-devel python-pip
```

There are also packaged versions of the clients available in RDO (https://www.rdoproject.org/) ↗ that enable yum to install the clients as described in *Section 4.2.2.2, "Installing from packages"*.

SUSE Linux Enterprise Server

A packaged version available in the Open Build Service (https://build.opensuse.org/package/show?package=python-pip&project=Cloud:OpenStack:Master (https://build.opensuse.org/package/show?package=python-pip&project=Cloud:OpenStack.Master) ↗) **enables you to use** YaST or zypper to install the package.

Prerequisite	Description
	First, add the Open Build Service repository:

```
# zypper addrepo -f obs://Cloud:OpenStack: \
Liberty/SLE_12 Liberty
```

Then install pip and use it to manage client installation:

```
# zypper install python-devel python-pip
```

There are also packaged versions of the clients available that enable zypper to install the clients as described in *Section 4.2.2.2, "Installing from packages"*.

openSUSE

You can install pip and use it to manage client installation:

```
# zypper install python-devel python-pip
```

There are also packaged versions of the clients available that enable zypper to install the clients as described in *Section 4.2.2.2, "Installing from packages"*.

4.2.2   Install the OpenStack client

The following example shows the command for installing the OpenStack client with `pip`, which supports multiple services.

```
# pip install python-openstackclient
```

The following clients, while valid, are de-emphasized in favor of a common client. Instead of installing and learning all these clients, we recommend installing and using the OpenStack client. You may need to install an individual project's client because coverage is not yet sufficient in the OpenStack client. If you need to install an individual client's project, replace the `<project>` name in this `pip install` command using the list below.

```
# pip install python-<project>client
```

- `barbican` - Key Manager Service API

- `ceilometer` - Telemetry API

- `cinder` - Block Storage API and extensions

- `cloudkitty` - Rating service API

- `designate` - DNS service API

- `fuel` - Deployment service API

- `glance` - Image service API

- `gnocchi` - Telemetry API v3

- `heat` - Orchestration API

- `magnum` - Containers service API

- `manila` - Shared file systems API

- `mistral` - Workflow service API

- `monasca` - Monitoring API

- `murano` - Application catalog API

- `neutron` - Networking API

- `nova` - Compute API and extensions

- `sahara` - Data Processing API

- `senlin` - Clustering service API

- `swift` - Object Storage API

- `trove` - Database service API

- `openstack` - Common OpenStack client supporting multiple services

The following CLIs are deprecated in favor of `openstack`, the Common OpenStack client supporting multiple services:

- `keystone` - Identity service API and extensions

While you can install the `keystone` client for interacting with version 2.0 of the service's API, you should use the `openstack` client for all Identity interactions.

4.2.2.1 Installing with pip

Use pip to install the OpenStack clients on a Linux, Mac OS X, or Microsoft Windows system. It is easy to use and ensures that you get the latest version of the client from the Python Package Index (https://pypi.python.org/pypi) ↗. Also, pip enables you to update or remove a package. Install each client separately by using the following command:

- For Mac OS X or Linux:

```
# pip install python-PROJECTclient
```

- For Microsoft Windows:

```
C:\>pip install python-PROJECTclient
```

4.2.2.2 Installing from packages

RDO, openSUSE, SUSE Linux Enterprise, Debian, and Ubuntu have client packages that can be installed without `pip`.

- On Red Hat Enterprise Linux, CentOS, or Fedora, use `yum` to install the clients from the packaged versions available in RDO (https://www.rdoproject.org/) ↗:

```
# yum install python-PROJECTclient
```

- For Ubuntu or Debian, use `apt-get` to install the clients from the packaged versions:

```
# apt-get install python-PROJECTclient
```

- For openSUSE, use `zypper` to install the clients from the distribution packages service:

```
# zypper install python-PROJECTclient
```

- For SUSE Linux Enterprise Server, use `zypper` to install the clients from the distribution packages in the Open Build Service. First, add the Open Build Service repository:

```
# zypper addrepo -f obs://Cloud:OpenStack:Liberty/SLE_12 Liberty
```

Then you can install the packages:

```
# zypper install python-PROJECTclient
```

4.2.3   Upgrade or remove clients

To upgrade a client, add the --upgrade option to the **pip install** command:

```
# pip install --upgrade python-PROJECTclient
```

To remove the client, run the **pip uninstall** command:

```
# pip uninstall python-PROJECTclient
```

4.2.4   What's next

Before you can run client commands, you must create and source the PROJECT-openrc.sh file to set environment variables. See .

4.3   Discover the version number for a client

Run the following command to discover the version number for a client:

```
$ PROJECT --version
```

For example, to see the version number for the nova client, run the following command:

```
$ nova --version
2.31.0
```

4.4 Set environment variables using the OpenStack RC file

To set the required environment variables for the OpenStack command-line clients, you must create an environment file called an OpenStack rc file, or `openrc.sh` file. If your OpenStack installation provides it, you can download the file from the OpenStack dashboard as an administrative user or any other user. This project-specific environment file contains the credentials that all OpenStack services use.

When you source the file, environment variables are set for your current shell. The variables enable the OpenStack client commands to communicate with the OpenStack services that run in the cloud.

 Note

Defining environment variables using an environment file is not a common practice on Microsoft Windows. Environment variables are usually defined in the *Advanced › System Properties* dialog box.

4.4.1 Download and source the OpenStack RC file

1. Log in to the OpenStack dashboard, choose the project for which you want to download the OpenStack RC file, on the *Project* tab, open the *Compute* tab and click *Access & Security*.

2. On the *API Access* tab, click *Download OpenStack RC File* and save the file. The filename will be of the form `PROJECT-openrc.sh` where `PROJECT` is the name of the project for which you downloaded the file.

3. Copy the `PROJECT-openrc.sh` file to the computer from which you want to run OpenStack commands.
   For example, copy the file to the computer from which you want to upload an image with a `glance` client command.

4. On any shell from which you want to run OpenStack commands, source the `PROJECT-openrc.sh` file for the respective project.

In the following example, the `demo-openrc.sh` file is sourced for the demo project:

```
$ source demo-openrc.sh
```

5. When you are prompted for an OpenStack password, enter the password for the user who downloaded the `PROJECT-openrc.sh` file.

4.4.2 Create and source the OpenStack RC file

Alternatively, you can create the `PROJECT-openrc.sh` file from scratch, if you cannot download the file from the dashboard.

1. In a text editor, create a file named `PROJECT-openrc.sh` and add the following authentication information:

```
export OS_USERNAME=username
export OS_PASSWORD=password
export OS_TENANT_NAME=projectName
export OS_AUTH_URL=https://identityHost:portNumber/v2.0
# The following lines can be omitted
export OS_TENANT_ID=tenantIDString
export OS_REGION_NAME=regionName
export OS_CACERT=/path/to/cacertFile
```

2. On any shell from which you want to run OpenStack commands, source the `PROJECT-openrc.sh` file for the respective project. In this example, you source the `admin-openrc.sh` file for the admin project:

```
$ source admin-openrc.sh
```

 Note

You are not prompted for the password with this method. The password lives in clear text format in the `PROJECT-openrc.sh` file. Restrict the permissions on this file to avoid security problems. You can also remove the `OS_PASSWORD` variable from the file, and use the `--password` parameter with OpenStack client commands instead.

Note

You must set the OS_CACERT environment variable when using the https protocol in the OS_AUTH_URL environment setting because the verification process for the TLS (HTTPS) server certificate uses the one indicated in the environment. This certificate will be used when verifying the TLS (HTTPS) server certificate.

4.4.3 Override environment variable values

When you run OpenStack client commands, you can override some environment variable settings by using the options that are listed at the end of the help output of the various client commands. For example, you can override the OS_PASSWORD setting in the PROJECT-openrc.sh file by specifying a password on a **openstack** command, as follows:

```
$ openstack --os-password PASSWORD service list
```

Where PASSWORD is your password.

A user specifies their username and password credentials to interact with OpenStack, using any client command. These credentials can be specified using various mechanisms, namely, the environment variable or command-line argument. It is not safe to specify the password using either of these methods.

For example, when you specify your password using the command-line client with the --os-password argument, anyone with access to your computer can view it in plain text with the ps field.

To avoid storing the password in plain text, you can prompt for the OpenStack password interactively.

4.5 Manage projects, users, and roles

As a cloud administrator, you manage projects, users, and roles. Projects are organizational units in the cloud to which you can assign users. Projects are also known as tenants or accounts. Users can be members of one or more projects. Roles define which actions users can perform. You assign roles to user-project pairs.

You can define actions for OpenStack service roles in the `/etc/PROJECT/policy.json` files. For example, define actions for Compute service roles in the `/etc/nova/policy.json` file.

You can manage projects, users, and roles independently from each other.

During cloud set up, the operator defines at least one project, user, and role.

Learn how to add, update, and delete projects and users, assign users to one or more projects, and change or remove the assignment. To enable or temporarily disable a project or user, you update that project or user. You can also change quotas at the project level.

Before you can delete a user account, you must remove the user account from its primary project.

Before you can run client commands, you must download and source an OpenStack RC file. See Download and source the OpenStack RC file (http://docs.openstack.org/user-guide/common/cli_set_environment_variables_using_openstack_rc.html#download-and-source-the-openstack-rc-file) ↗.

4.5.1   Projects

A project is a group of zero or more users. In Compute, a project owns virtual machines. In Object Storage, a project owns containers. Users can be associated with more than one project. Each project and user pairing can have a role associated with it.

4.5.1.1   List projects

List all projects with their ID, name, and whether they are enabled or disabled:

```
$ openstack project list
+----------------------------------+-------------------+
| id                               | name              |
+----------------------------------+-------------------+
| f7ac731cc11f40efbc03a9f9e1d1d21f | admin             |
| c150ab41f0d9443f8874e32e725a4cc8 | alt_demo          |
| a9debfe41a6d4d09a677da737b907d5e | demo              |
| 9208739195a34c628c58c95d157917d7 | invisible_to_admin |
| 3943a53dc92a49b2827fae94363851e1 | service           |
| 80cab5e1f02045abad92a2864cfd76cb | test_project      |
+----------------------------------+-------------------+
```

4.5.1.2 Create a project

Create a project named `new-project`:

```
$ openstack project create --description 'my new project' new-project
+-------------+----------------------------------+
| Field       | Value                            |
+-------------+----------------------------------+
| description | my new project                   |
| enabled     | True                             |
| id          | 1a4a0618b306462c9830f876b0bd6af2 |
| name        | new-project                      |
+-------------+----------------------------------+
```

4.5.1.3 Update a project

Specify the project ID to update a project. You can update the name, description, and enabled status of a project.

- To temporarily disable a project:

```
$ openstack project set PROJECT_ID --disable
```

- To enable a disabled project:

```
$ openstack project set PROJECT_ID --enable
```

- To update the name of a project:

```
$ openstack project set PROJECT_ID --name project-new
```

- To verify your changes, show information for the updated project:

```
$ openstack project show PROJECT_ID
+-------------+----------------------------------+
| Field       | Value                            |
+-------------+----------------------------------+
| description | my new project                   |
```

```
| enabled    | True                             |
| id         | 1a4a0618b306462c9830f876b0bd6af2 |
| name       | project-new                      |
+------------+----------------------------------+
```

4.5.1.4   Delete a project

Specify the project ID to delete a project:

```
$ openstack project delete PROJECT_ID
```

4.5.2   User

4.5.2.1   List users

List all users:

```
$ openstack user list
+----------------------------------+--------+
| id                               | name   |
+----------------------------------+--------+
| 352b37f5c89144d4ad0534139266d51f | admin  |
| 86c0de739bcb4802b8dc786921355813 | demo   |
| 32ec34aae8ea432e8af560a1cec0e881 | glance |
| 7047fcb7908e420cb36e13bbd72c972c | nova   |
+----------------------------------+--------+
```

4.5.2.2   Create a user

To create a user, you must specify a name. Optionally, you can specify a tenant ID, password, and email address. It is recommended that you include the tenant ID and password because the user cannot log in to the dashboard without this information.

Create the `new-user` user:

```
$ openstack user create --project new-project --password PASSWORD new-user
+-----------+----------------------------------+
| Field     | Value                            |
+-----------+----------------------------------+
| email     |                                  |
| enabled   | True                             |
| id        | 6e5140962b424cb9814fb172889d3be2 |
| name      | new-user                         |
| tenantId  | new-project                      |
+-----------+----------------------------------+
```

4.5.2.3 Update a user

You can update the name, email address, and enabled status for a user.

- To temporarily disable a user account:

```
$ openstack user set USER_NAME --disable
```

If you disable a user account, the user cannot log in to the dashboard. However, data for the user account is maintained, so you can enable the user at any time.

- To enable a disabled user account:

```
$ openstack user set USER_NAME --enable
```

- To change the name and description for a user account:

```
$ openstack user set USER_NAME --name user-new --email new-user@example.com
User has been updated.
```

4.5.2.4 Delete a user

Delete a specified user account:

```
$ openstack user delete USER_NAME
```

4.5.3 Roles and role assignments

4.5.3.1 List available roles

List the available roles:

```
$ openstack role list
+----------------------------------+--------------+
| id                               | name         |
+----------------------------------+--------------+
| 71ccc37d41c8491c975ae72676db687f | Member       |
| 149f50a1fe684bfa88dae76a48d26ef7 | ResellerAdmin |
| 9fe2ff9ee4384b1894a90878d3e92bab | _member_     |
| 6ecf391421604da985db2f141e46a7c8 | admin        |
| deb4fffd123c4d02a907c2c74559dccf | anotherrole  |
+----------------------------------+--------------+
```

4.5.3.2 Create a role

Users can be members of multiple projects. To assign users to multiple projects, define a role and assign that role to a user-project pair.

Create the new-role role:

```
$ openstack role create new-role
+--------+----------------------------------+
| Field  | Value                            |
+--------+----------------------------------+
| id     | bef1f95537914b1295da6aa038ef4de6 |
```

```
| name    | new-role                              |
+---------+---------------------------------------+
```

4.5.3.3 Assign a role

To assign a user to a project, you must assign the role to a user-project pair. To do this, you need the user, role, and project IDs.

1. List users and note the user ID you want to assign to the role:

```
$ openstack user list
+----------------------------------+----------+---------+----------------------
+
| id                               | name     | enabled | email
 |
+----------------------------------+----------+---------+----------------------
+
| 352b37f5c89144d4ad0534139266d51f | admin    | True    | admin@example.com
 |
| 981422ec906d4842b2fc2a8658a5b534 | alt_demo | True    | alt_demo@example.com
 |
| 036e22a764ae497992f5fb8e9fd79896 | cinder   | True    | cinder@example.com
 |
| 86c0de739bcb4802b8dc786921355813 | demo     | True    | demo@example.com
 |
| 32ec34aae8ea432e8af560a1cec0e881 | glance   | True    | glance@example.com
 |
| 7047fcb7908e420cb36e13bbd72c972c | nova     | True    | nova@example.com
 |
+----------------------------------+----------+---------+----------------------
+
```

2. List role IDs and note the role ID you want to assign:

```
$ openstack role list
+----------------------------------+---------------+
```

```
| id                               | name         |
+----------------------------------+--------------+
| 71ccc37d41c8491c975ae72676db687f | Member       |
| 149f50a1fe684bfa88dae76a48d26ef7 | ResellerAdmin|
| 9fe2ff9ee4384b1894a90878d3e92bab | _member_     |
| 6ecf391421604da985db2f141e46a7c8 | admin        |
| deb4fffd123c4d02a907c2c74559dccf | anotherrole  |
| bef1f95537914b1295da6aa038ef4de6 | new-role     |
+----------------------------------+--------------+
```

3. List projects and note the project ID you want to assign to the role:

```
$ openstack project list
+----------------------------------+------------------+---------+
| id                               | name             | enabled |
+----------------------------------+------------------+---------+
| f7ac731cc11f40efbc03a9f9e1d1d21f | admin            |  True   |
| c150ab41f0d9443f8874e32e725a4cc8 | alt_demo         |  True   |
| a9debfe41a6d4d09a677da737b907d5e | demo             |  True   |
| 9208739195a34c628c58c95d157917d7 | invisible_to_admin |  True |
| caa9b4ce7d5c4225aa25d6ff8b35c31f | new-user         |  True   |
| 1a4a0618b306462c9830f876b0bd6af2 | project-new      |  True   |
| 3943a53dc92a49b2827fae94363851e1 | service          |  True   |
| 80cab5e1f02045abad92a2864cfd76cb | test_project     |  True   |
+----------------------------------+------------------+---------+
```

4. Assign a role to a user-project pair. In this example, assign the new-role role to the demo and test-project pair:

```
$ openstack role add --user USER_NAME --project TENANT_ID ROLE_NAME
```

5. Verify the role assignment:

```
$ openstack role list --user USER_NAME --project TENANT_ID
+---------------+-----------+---------------------------+---------------+
| id            | name      | user_id                   | tenant_id     |
+---------------+-----------+---------------------------+---------------+
```

```
| bef1f9553... | new-role | 86c0de739bcb4802b21355... | 80cab5e1f... |
+--------------+----------+---------------------------+--------------+
```

4.5.3.4   View role details

View details for a specified role:

```
$ openstack role show ROLE_NAME
+----------+----------------------------------+
| Field    | Value                            |
+----------+----------------------------------+
| id       | bef1f95537914b1295da6aa038ef4de6 |
| name     | new-role                         |
+----------+----------------------------------+
```

4.5.3.5   Remove a role

Remove a role from a user-project pair:

1. Run the **openstack role remove** command:

   ```
   $ openstack role remove --user USER_NAME --project TENANT_ID ROLE_NAME
   ```

2. Verify the role removal:

   ```
   $ openstack role list --user USER_NAME --project TENANT_ID
   ```

   If the role was removed, the command output omits the removed role.

4.6   Manage project security

Security groups are sets of IP filter rules that are applied to all project instances, which define networking access to the instance. Group rules are project specific; project members can edit the default rules for their group and add new rule sets.

All projects have a `default` security group which is applied to any instance that has no other defined security group. Unless you change the default, this security group denies all incoming traffic and allows only outgoing traffic to your instance.

You can use the `allow_same_net_traffic` option in the `/etc/nova/nova.conf` file to globally control whether the rules apply to hosts which share a network.

If set to:

- `True` (default), hosts on the same subnet are not filtered and are allowed to pass all types of traffic between them. On a flat network, this allows all instances from all projects unfiltered communication. With VLAN networking, this allows access between instances within the same project. You can also simulate this setting by configuring the default security group to allow all traffic from the subnet.

- `False`, security groups are enforced for all connections.

Additionally, the number of maximum rules per security group is controlled by the `security_group_rules` and the number of allowed security groups per project is controlled by the `security_groups` quota (see the Manage quotas (http://docs.openstack.org/user-guide-admin/cli_set_quotas.html) ↗ section).

4.6.1 List and view current security groups

From the command-line you can get a list of security groups for the project, using the **nova** command:

1. Ensure your system variables are set for the user and tenant for which you are checking security group rules. For example:

```
export OS_USERNAME=demo00
export OS_TENANT_NAME=tenant01
```

2. Output security groups, as follows:

```
$ nova secgroup-list
+---------+-------------+
| Name    | Description |
+---------+-------------+
```

```
| default | default   |
| open    | all ports |
+---------+-----------+
```

3. View the details of a group, as follows:

```
$ nova secgroup-list-rules groupName
```

For example:

```
$ nova secgroup-list-rules open
+-------------+-----------+---------+-----------+--------------+
| IP Protocol | From Port | To Port | IP Range  | Source Group |
+-------------+-----------+---------+-----------+--------------+
| icmp        | -1        | 255     | 0.0.0.0/0 |              |
| tcp         | 1         | 65535   | 0.0.0.0/0 |              |
| udp         | 1         | 65535   | 0.0.0.0/0 |              |
+-------------+-----------+---------+-----------+--------------+
```

These rules are allow type rules as the default is deny. The first column is the IP protocol
(one of icmp, tcp, or udp). The second and third columns specify the affected port range.
The third column specifies the IP range in CIDR format. This example shows the full port
range for all protocols allowed from all IPs.

4.6.2 Create a security group

When adding a new security group, you should pick a descriptive but brief name. This name
shows up in brief descriptions of the instances that use it where the longer description field
often does not. For example, seeing that an instance is using security group "http" is much easier
to understand than "bobs_group" or "secgrp1".

1. Ensure your system variables are set for the user and tenant for which you are creating
   security group rules.

2. Add the new security group, as follows:

```
$ nova secgroup-create GroupName Description
```

For example:

```
$ nova secgroup-create global_http "Allows Web traffic anywhere on the Internet."
+-----------------------------------------+--------------
+-------------------------------------------+
| Id                                      | Name        | Description
         |
+-----------------------------------------+--------------
+-------------------------------------------+
| 1578a08c-5139-4f3e-9012-86bd9dd9f23b | global_http | Allows Web traffic anywhere on the
 Internet. |
+-----------------------------------------+--------------
+-------------------------------------------+
```

3. Add a new group rule, as follows:

```
$ nova secgroup-add-rule secGroupName ip-protocol from-port to-port CIDR
```

The arguments are positional, and the `from port` and `to-port` arguments specify the local port range connections are allowed to access, not the source and destination ports of the connection. For example:

```
$ nova secgroup-add-rule global_http tcp 80 80 0.0.0.0/0
+-------------+-----------+---------+-----------+--------------+
| IP Protocol | From Port | To Port | IP Range  | Source Group |
+-------------+-----------+---------+-----------+--------------+
| tcp         | 80        | 80      | 0.0.0.0/0 |              |
+-------------+-----------+---------+-----------+--------------+
```

You can create complex rule sets by creating additional rules. For example, if you want to pass both HTTP and HTTPS traffic, run:

```
$ nova secgroup-add-rule global_http tcp 443 443 0.0.0.0/0
+-------------+-----------+---------+-----------+--------------+
| IP Protocol | From Port | To Port | IP Range  | Source Group |
+-------------+-----------+---------+-----------+--------------+
| tcp         | 443       | 443     | 0.0.0.0/0 |              |
```

```
+-------------+-----------+---------+-----------+-------------+
```

Despite only outputting the newly added rule, this operation is additive (both rules are created and enforced).

4. View all rules for the new security group, as follows:

```
$ nova secgroup-list-rules global_http
+-------------+-----------+---------+-----------+--------------+
| IP Protocol | From Port | To Port | IP Range  | Source Group |
+-------------+-----------+---------+-----------+--------------+
| tcp         | 80        | 80      | 0.0.0.0/0 |              |
| tcp         | 443       | 443     | 0.0.0.0/0 |              |
+-------------+-----------+---------+-----------+--------------+
```

4.6.3 Delete a security group

1. Ensure your system variables are set for the user and tenant for which you are deleting a security group.

2. Delete the new security group, as follows:

```
$ nova secgroup-delete GroupName
```

For example:

```
$ nova secgroup-delete global_http
```

4.6.4 Create security group rules for a cluster of instances

Source Groups are a special, dynamic way of defining the CIDR of allowed sources. The user specifies a Source Group (Security Group name), and all the user's other Instances using the specified Source Group are selected dynamically. This alleviates the need for individual rules to allow each new member of the cluster.

1. Make sure to set the system variables for the user and tenant for which you are creating a security group rule.

2. Add a source group, as follows:

```
$ nova secgroup-add-group-rule secGroupName source-group ip-protocol from-port to-port
```

For example:

```
$ nova secgroup-add-group-rule cluster global_http tcp 22 22
```

The `cluster` rule allows ssh access from any other instance that uses the `global_http` group.

4.7 Manage services

4.7.1 Create and manage services and service users

The Identity service enables you to define services, as follows:

- Service catalog template. The Identity service acts as a service catalog of endpoints for other OpenStack services. The `etc/default_catalog.templates` template file defines the endpoints for services. When the Identity service uses a template file back end, any changes that are made to the endpoints are cached. These changes do not persist when you restart the service or reboot the machine.

- An SQL back end for the catalog service. When the Identity service is online, you must add the services to the catalog. When you deploy a system for production, use the SQL back end.

The `auth_token` middleware supports the use of either a shared secret or users for each service.

To authenticate users against the Identity service, you must create a service user for each OpenStack service. For example, create a service user for the Compute, Block Storage, and Networking services.

To configure the OpenStack services with service users, create a project for all services and create users for each service. Assign the admin role to each service user and project pair. This role enables users to validate tokens and authenticate and authorize other user requests.

4.7.1.1 Create a service

1. List the available services:

```
$ openstack service list
+-------------------------------------+----------+------------+
| ID                                  | Name     | Type       |
+-------------------------------------+----------+------------+
| 9816f1faaa7c4842b90fb4821cd09223    | cinder   | volume     |
| 1250f64f31e34dcd9a93d35a075ddbe1    | cinderv2 | volumev2   |
| da8cf9f8546b4a428c43d5e032fe4afc    | ec2      | ec2        |
| 5f105eeb55924b7290c8675ad7e294ae    | glance   | image      |
| dcaa566e912e4c0e900dc86804e3dde0    | keystone | identity   |
| 4a715cfbc3664e9ebf388534ff2be76a    | nova     | compute    |
| 1aed4a6cf7274297ba4026cf5d5e96c5    | novav21  | computev21 |
| bed063c790634c979778551f66c8ede9    | neutron  | network    |
| 6feb2e0b98874d88bee221974770e372    |    s3     |     s3     |
+-------------------------------------+----------+------------+
```

2. To create a service, run this command:

```
$ openstack service create --name SERVICE_NAME --description SERVICE_DESCRIPTION
  SERVICE_TYPE
```

The arguments are:

- `service_name`: the unique name of the new service.

- `service_type`: the service type, such as `identity`, `compute`, `network`, image, `object-store` or any other service identifier string.

- `service_description`: the description of the service.

For example, to create a `swift` service of type `object-store`, run this command:

```
$ openstack service create --name swift --description "object store service" object-store
+-------------+-----------------------------------+
| Field       | Value                             |
+-------------+-----------------------------------+
```

```
| description | object store service          |
| enabled     | True                          |
| id          | 84c23f4b942c44c38b9c42c5e517cd9a |
| name        | swift                         |
| type        | object-store                  |
+-------------+-------------------------------+
```

3. To get details for a service, run this command:

```
$ openstack service show SERVICE_TYPE|SERVICE_NAME|SERVICE_ID
```

For example:

```
$ openstack service show object-store
+-------------+-------------------------------------+
| Field       | Value                               |
+-------------+-------------------------------------+
| description | object store service                |
| enabled     | True                                |
| id          | 84c23f4b942c44c38b9c42c5e517cd9a    |
| name        | swift                               |
| type        | object-store                        |
+-------------+-------------------------------------+
```

4.7.1.2   Create service users

1. Create a project for the service users. Typically, this project is named `service`, but choose any name you like:

```
$ openstack project create service
+-------------+-------------------------------------+
| Field       | Value                               |
+-------------+-------------------------------------+
| description | None                                |
| enabled     | True                                |
| id          | 3e9f3f5399624b2db548d7f871bd5322    |
```

```
| name        | service                      |
+-------------+------------------------------+
```

2. Create service users for the relevant services for your deployment.

3. Assign the admin role to the user-project pair.

```
$ openstack role add --project service --user SERVICE_USER_NAME admin
+--------+----------------------------------+
| Field  | Value                            |
+--------+----------------------------------+
| id     | 233109e756c1465292f31e7662b429b1 |
| name   | admin                            |
+--------+----------------------------------+
```

4.7.1.3 Delete a service

To delete a specified service, specify its ID.

```
$ openstack service delete SERVICE_TYPE|SERVICE_NAME|SERVICE_ID
```

For example:

```
$ openstack service delete object-store
```

4.7.2 Manage Compute services

You can enable and disable Compute services. The following examples disable and enable the nova-compute service.

1. List the Compute services:

```
$ nova service-list
+------------------+----------+----------+---------+-------+----------------------------
+-----------------+
| Binary           | Host     | Zone     | Status  | State | Updated_at
 Disabled Reason |
```

```
+-----------------+----------+----------+----------+-------+----------------------------
+-----------------+
| nova-conductor  | devstack | internal | enabled | up    | 2013-10-16T00:56:08.000000 |
 None             |
| nova-cert       | devstack | internal | enabled | up    | 2013-10-16T00:56:09.000000 |
 None             |
| nova-compute    | devstack | nova     | enabled | up    | 2013-10-16T00:56:07.000000 |
 None             |
| nova-network    | devstack | internal | enabled | up    | 2013-10-16T00:56:06.000000 |
 None             |
| nova-scheduler  | devstack | internal | enabled | up    | 2013-10-16T00:56:04.000000 |
 None             |
| nova-consoleauth | devstack | internal | enabled | up   | 2013-10-16T00:56:07.000000 |
 None             |
+-----------------+----------+----------+----------+-------+----------------------------
+-----------------+
```

2. Disable a nova service:

```
$ nova service-disable localhost.localdomain nova-compute --reason 'trial log'
+----------+--------------+----------+-------------------+
| Host     | Binary       | Status   | Disabled Reason   |
+----------+--------------+----------+-------------------+
| devstack | nova-compute | disabled | Trial log         |
+----------+--------------+----------+-------------------+
```

3. Check the service list:

```
$ nova service-list
+-----------------+----------+----------+----------+-------+----------------------------
+-----------------+
| Binary          | Host     | Zone     | Status   | State | Updated_at
 | Disabled Reason |
+-----------------+----------+----------+----------+-------+----------------------------
+-----------------+
| nova-conductor  | devstack | internal | enabled  | up    | 2013-10-16T00:56:48.000000
 | None            |
```

```
| nova-cert        | devstack | internal | enabled  | up   | 2013-10-16T00:56:49.000000
  | None            |
| nova-compute     | devstack | nova     | disabled | up   | 2013-10-16T00:56:47.000000
  | Trial log       |
| nova-network     | devstack | internal | enabled  | up   | 2013-10-16T00:56:51.000000
  | None            |
| nova-scheduler   | devstack | internal | enabled  | up   | 2013-10-16T00:56:44.000000
  | None            |
| nova-consoleauth | devstack | internal | enabled  | up   | 2013-10-16T00:56:47.000000
  | None            |
+------------------+----------+----------+----------+------+----------------------------
+------------------+
```

4. Enable the service:

```
$ nova service-enable localhost.localdomain nova-compute
+----------+--------------+---------+
| Host     | Binary       | Status  |
+----------+--------------+---------+
| devstack | nova-compute | enabled |
+----------+--------------+---------+
```

5. Check the service list:

```
$ nova service-list
+------------------+----------+----------+----------+-------+----------------------------
+------------------+
| Binary           | Host     | Zone     | Status   | State | Updated_at                 |
  Disabled Reason |
+------------------+----------+----------+----------+-------+----------------------------
+------------------+
| nova-conductor   | devstack | internal | enabled  | up    | 2013-10-16T00:57:08.000000 |
  None             |
| nova-cert        | devstack | internal | enabled  | up    | 2013-10-16T00:57:09.000000 |
  None             |
| nova-compute     | devstack | nova     | enabled  | up    | 2013-10-16T00:57:07.000000 |
  None             |
```

```
| nova-network    | devstack | internal | enabled | up     | 2013-10-16T00:57:11.000000 |
  None             |
| nova-scheduler  | devstack | internal | enabled | up     | 2013-10-16T00:57:14.000000 |
  None             |
| nova-consoleauth | devstack | internal | enabled | up     | 2013-10-16T00:57:07.000000 |
  None             |
+-----------------+----------+----------+---------+--------+----------------------------
+-----------------+
```

4.8   Manage images

The cloud operator assigns roles to users. Roles determine who can upload and manage images. The operator might restrict image upload and management to only cloud administrators or operators.

You can upload images through the `glance` client or the Image service API. You can use the `nova` client for the image management. The latter provides mechanisms to list and delete images, set and delete image metadata, and create images of a running instance or snapshot and backup types.

After you upload an image, you cannot change it.

For details about image creation, see the Virtual Machine Image Guide (http://docs.openstack.org/image-guide/) ↗.

4.8.1   List or get details for images (glance)

To get a list of images and to get further details about a single image, use **glance image-list** and **glance image-show** commands.

```
$ glance image-list
+----------+-----------------------------------------+-------------+------------------+----------
+--------+
| ID       | Name                                    | Disk Format | Container Format | Size     |
  Status |
+----------+-----------------------------------------+-------------+------------------+----------
+--------+
```

```
| 397e7... | cirros-0.3.2-x86_64-uec        | ami | ami | 25165824 |
  active |
| df430... | cirros-0.3.2-x86_64-uec-kernel | aki | aki | 4955792  |
  active |
| 3cf85... | cirros-0.3.2-x86_64-uec-ramdisk | ari | ari | 3714968  |
  active |
| 7e514... | myCirrosImage                  | ami | ami | 14221312 |
  active |
+----------+--------------------------------+---------------+------------------+----------
+--------+
```

```
$ glance image-show myCirrosImage
+-----------------------------------------+-------------------------------------------+
| Property                                | Value                                     |
+-----------------------------------------+-------------------------------------------+
| Property 'base_image_ref'               | 397e713c-b95b-4186-ad46-6126863ea0a9      |
| Property 'image_location'               | snapshot                                  |
| Property 'image_state'                  | available                                 |
| Property 'image_type'                   | snapshot                                  |
| Property 'instance_type_ephemeral_gb'   | 0                                         |
| Property 'instance_type_flavorid'       | 2                                         |
| Property 'instance_type_id'             | 5                                         |
| Property 'instance_type_memory_mb'      | 2048                                      |
| Property 'instance_type_name'           | m1.small                                  |
| Property 'instance_type_root_gb'        | 20                                        |
| Property 'instance_type_rxtx_factor'    | 1                                         |
| Property 'instance_type_swap'           | 0                                         |
| Property 'instance_type_vcpu_weight'    | None                                      |
| Property 'instance_type_vcpus'          | 1                                         |
| Property 'instance_uuid'                | 84c6e57d-a6b1-44b6-81eb-fcb36afd31b5      |
| Property 'kernel_id'                    | df430cc2-3406-4061-b635-a51c16e488ac      |
| Property 'owner_id'                     | 66265572db174a7aa66eba661f58eb9e          |
| Property 'ramdisk_id'                   | 3cf852bd-2332-48f4-9ae4-7d926d50945e      |
| Property 'user_id'                      | 376744b5910b4b4da7d8e6cb483b06a8          |
| checksum                                | 8e4838effa1969ad591655d6485c7ba8          |
| container_format                        | ami                                       |
```

```
| created_at    | 2013-07-22T19:45:58                  |
| deleted       | False                                |
| disk_format   | ami                                  |
| id            | 7e5142af-1253-4634-bcc6-89482c5f2e8a |
| is_public     | False                                |
| min_disk      | 0                                    |
| min_ram       | 0                                    |
| name          | myCirrosImage                        |
| owner         | 66265572db174a7aa66eba661f58eb9e     |
| protected     | False                                |
| size          | 14221312                             |
| status        | active                               |
| updated_at    | 2013-07-22T19:46:42                  |
+---------------------------------------+--------------------------------------+
```

When viewing a list of images, you can also use grep to filter the list, as follows:

```
$ glance image-list | grep 'cirros'
| 397e713c-b95b-4186-ad46-612... | cirros-0.3.2-x86_64-uec         | ami | ami | 25165824 |
active |
| df430cc2-3406-4061-b635-a51... | cirros-0.3.2-x86_64-uec-kernel  | aki | aki | 4955792  |
active |
| 3cf852bd-2332-48f4-9ae4-7d9... | cirros-0.3.2-x86_64-uec-ramdisk | ari | ari | 3714968  |
active |
```

 Note

To store location metadata for images, which enables direct file access for a client, update the /etc/glance/glance-api.conf file with the following statements:

- show_multiple_locations = True

- filesystem_store_metadata_file = filePath, where filePath points to a JSON file that defines the mount point for OpenStack images on your system and a unique ID. For example:

```
[{
    "id": "2d9bb53f-70ea-4066-a68b-67960eaae673",
```

```
      "mountpoint": "/var/lib/glance/images/"
}]
```

After you restart the Image service, you can use the following syntax to view the image's location information:

```
$ glance --os-image-api-version 2 image-show imageID
```

For example, using the image ID shown above, you would issue the command as follows:

```
$ glance --os-image-api-version 2 image-show 2d9bb53f-70ea-4066-
a68b-67960eaae673
```

4.8.2   Create or update an image (glance)

To create an image, use **glance image-create**:

```
$ glance image-create imageName
```

To update an image by name or ID, use **glance image-update**:

```
$ glance image-update imageName
```

The following list explains the optional arguments that you can use with the `create` and `up-`
`date` commands to modify image properties. For more information, refer to Image service
chapter in the OpenStack Command-Line Interface Reference (http://docs.openstack.org/cli-refer-
ence/index.html) ↗.

`--name NAME`

The name of the image.

`--disk-format DISK_FORMAT`

The disk format of the image. Acceptable formats are ami, ari, aki, vhd, vmdk, raw, qcow2,
vdi, and iso.

`--container-format CONTAINER_FORMAT`

The container format of the image. Acceptable formats are ami, ari, aki, bare, docker, and
ovf.

`--owner TENANT_ID --size SIZE`

> The tenant who should own the image. The size of image data, in bytes.

`--min-disk DISK_GB`

> The minimum size of the disk needed to boot the image, in gigabytes.

`--min-ram DISK_RAM`

> The minimum amount of RAM needed to boot the image, in megabytes.

`--location IMAGE_URL`

> The URL where the data for this image resides. For example, if the image data is stored in swift, you could specify `swift://account:key@example.com/container/obj`.

`--file FILE`

> Local file that contains the disk image to be uploaded during the update. Alternatively, you can pass images to the client through stdin.

`--checksum CHECKSUM`

> Hash of image data to use for verification.

`--copy from IMAGE_URL`

> Similar to `--location` in usage, but indicates that the image server should immediately copy the data and store it in its configured image store.

`--is-public [True|False]`

> Makes an image accessible for all the tenants (admin-only by default).

`--is-protected [True|False]`

> Prevents an image from being deleted.

`--property KEY=VALUE`

> Arbitrary property to associate with image. This option can be used multiple times.

`--purge-props`

> Deletes all image properties that are not explicitly set in the update request. Otherwise, those properties not referenced are preserved.

`--human-readable`

> Prints the image size in a human-friendly format.

The following example shows the command that you would use to upload a CentOS 6.3 image in qcow2 format and configure it for public access:

```
$ glance image-create --name centos63-image --disk-format qcow2 \
  --container-format bare --is-public True --file ./centos63.qcow2
```

The following example shows how to update an existing image with a properties that describe the disk bus, the CD-ROM bus, and the VIF model:

 Note

When you use OpenStack with VMware vCenter Server, you need to specify the `vmware_disktype` and `vmware_adaptertype` properties with **glance image-create**. Also, we recommend that you set the `hypervisor_type="vmware"` property. For more information, see Images with VMware vSphere (http://docs.openstack.org/liberty/config-reference/content/vmware.html#VMware_images) ↗ in the *OpenStack Configuration Reference.*

```
$ glance image-update \
    --property hw_disk_bus=scsi \
    --property hw_cdrom_bus=ide \
    --property hw_vif_model=e1000 \
    f16-x86_64-openstack-sda
```

Currently the libvirt virtualization tool determines the disk, CD-ROM, and VIF device models based on the configured hypervisor type (`libvirt_type` in `/etc/nova/nova.conf` file). For the sake of optimal performance, libvirt defaults to using virtio for both disk and VIF (NIC) models. The disadvantage of this approach is that it is not possible to run operating systems that lack virtio drivers, for example, BSD, Solaris, and older versions of Linux and Windows.

If you specify a disk or CD-ROM bus model that is not supported, see the *Table 4.2, "Disk and CD-ROM bus model values"*. If you specify a VIF model that is not supported, the instance fails to launch. See the *Table 4.3, "VIF model values"*.

The valid model values depend on the `libvirt_type` setting, as shown in the following tables.

Disk and CD-ROM bus model values

TABLE 4.2: DISK AND CD-ROM BUS MODEL VALUES

libvirt_type setting	Supported model values
qemu or kvm	<ul><li>ide</li><li>scsi</li><li>virtio</li></ul>
xen	<ul><li>ide</li><li>xen</li></ul>

VIF model values

TABLE 4.3: VIF MODEL VALUES

libvirt_type setting	Supported model values
qemu or kvm	<ul><li>e1000</li><li>ne2k_pci</li><li>pcnet</li><li>rtl8139</li><li>virtio</li></ul>
xen	<ul><li>e1000</li><li>netfront</li><li>ne2k_pci</li><li>pcnet</li><li>rtl8139</li></ul>
vmware	<ul><li>VirtualE1000</li><li>VirtualPCNet32</li><li>VirtualVmxnet</li></ul>

4.8.3   Troubleshoot image creation

If you encounter problems in creating an image in the Image service or Compute, the following information may help you troubleshoot the creation process.

- Ensure that the version of qemu you are using is version 0.14 or later. Earlier versions of qemu result in an `unknown option -s` error message in the `nova-compute.log` file.

- Examine the `/var/log/nova-api.log` and `/var/log/nova-compute.log` log files for error messages.

4.9   Manage volumes

A volume is a detachable block storage device, similar to a USB hard drive. You can attach a volume to only one instance. To create and manage volumes, you use a combination of `nova` and `cinder` client commands.

4.9.1   Migrate a volume

As an administrator, you can migrate a volume with its data from one location to another in a manner that is transparent to users and workloads. You can migrate only detached volumes with no snapshots.

Possible use cases for data migration include:

- Bring down a physical storage device for maintenance without disrupting workloads.

- Modify the properties of a volume.

- Free up space in a thinly-provisioned back end.

Migrate a volume with the **cinder migrate** command, as shown in the following example:

```
$ cinder migrate volumeID destinationHost --force-host-copy True|False
```

In this example, `--force-host-copy True` forces the generic host-based migration mechanism and bypasses any driver optimizations.

Note

If the volume is in use or has snapshots, the specified host destination cannot accept the volume. If the user is not an administrator, the migration fails.

4.9.2   Create a volume

This example creates a `my-new-volume` volume based on an image.

1. List images, and note the ID of the image that you want to use for your volume:

```
$ nova image-list

+------------------------+------------------------------------+--------
+------------------------+
| ID                     | Name                               | Status | Server
      |
+========================+====================================+ |
+------------------------+
| 397e713c-b95b-4186...  | cirros-0.3.2-x86_64-uec            | ACTIVE |
      |
| df430cc2-3406-4061...  | cirros-0.3.2-x86_64-uec-kernel     | ACTIVE |
      |
| 3cf852bd-2332-48f4...  | cirros-0.3.2-x86_64-uec-ramdisk    | ACTIVE |
      |
| 7e5142af-1253-4634...  | myCirrosImage                      | ACTIVE | 84c6e57d-
a6b1-44b6-81... |
| 89bcd424-9d15-4723...  | mysnapshot                         | ACTIVE | f51ebd07-
c33d-4951-87... |
+------------------------+------------------------------------+--------
+------------------------+
```

2. List the availability zones, and note the ID of the availability zone in which you want to create your volume:

```
$ cinder availability-zone-list
```

```
+------+-----------+
| Name |  Status   |
+------+-----------+
| nova | available |
+------+-----------+
```

3. Create a volume with 8 gibibytes (GiB) of space, and specify the availability zone and image:

```
$ cinder create 8 --display-name my-new-volume --image-id 397e713c-b95b-4186-
ad46-6126863ea0a9 --availability-zone nova



+---------------------+--------------------------------------+
|      Property       |                Value                 |
+---------------------+--------------------------------------+
|     attachments     |                  []                  |
|  availability_zone  |                 nova                 |
|      bootable       |                false                 |
|     created_at      |      2013-07-25T17:02:12.472269       |
| display_description |                 None                 |
|    display_name     |            my-new-volume             |
|         id          | 573e024d-5235-49ce-8332-be1576d323f8 |
|      image_id       | 397e713c-b95b-4186-ad46-6126863ea0a9 |
|      metadata       |                  {}                  |
|        size         |                  8                   |
|     snapshot_id     |                 None                 |
|     source_volid    |                 None                 |
|       status        |               creating              |
|     volume_type     |                 None                 |
+---------------------+--------------------------------------+
```

4. To verify that your volume was created successfully, list the available volumes:

```
$ cinder list
```

```
+------------------+-----------+------------------+------+------------+----------
+-------------+
|     ID           |  Status   |  Display Name    | Size | Volume Type | Bootable |
 Attached to |
+------------------+-----------+------------------+------+------------+----------
+-------------+
| 573e024d-523... | available |  my-new-volume   |  8   |    None     |   true   |
     |
| bd7cf584-45d... | available |  my-bootable-vol |  8   |    None     |   true   |
     |
+------------------+-----------+------------------+------+------------+----------
+-------------+
```

If your volume was created successfully, its status is `available`. If its status is `error`, you might have exceeded your quota.

4.9.3   Attach a volume to an instance

1. Attach your volume to a server, specifying the server ID and the volume ID:

```
$ nova volume-attach 84c6e57d-a6b1-44b6-81eb-fcb36afd31b5 573e024d-5235-49ce-8332-
be1576d323f8 /dev/vdb


+----------+--------------------------------------+
| Property | Value                                |
+----------+--------------------------------------+
| device   | /dev/vdb                             |
| serverId | 84c6e57d-a6b1-44b6-81eb-fcb36afd31b5 |
| id       | 573e024d-5235-49ce-8332-be1576d323f8 |
| volumeId | 573e024d-5235-49ce-8332-be1576d323f8 |
+----------+--------------------------------------+
```

Note the ID of your volume.

2. Show information for your volume:

```
$ cinder show 573e024d-5235-49ce-8332-be1576d323f8
```

The output shows that the volume is attached to the server with ID 84c6e57d-a6b1-44b6-81eb-fcb36afd31b5, is in the nova availability zone, and is bootable.

```
+------------------------------+------------------------------------------------+
|           Property           |                     Value                      |
+------------------------------+------------------------------------------------+
|         attachments          |           [{u'device': u'/dev/vdb',            |
|                              |          u'server_id': u'84c6e57d-a            |
|                              |             u'id': u'573e024d-...              |
|                              |          u'volume_id': u'573e024d...           |
|       availability_zone      |                     nova                       |
|           bootable           |                     true                       |
|          created_at          |          2013-07-25T17:02:12.000000            |
|      display_description      |                     None                       |
|         display_name         |                 my-new-volume                  |
|              id              |    573e024d-5235-49ce-8332-be1576d323f8         |
|           metadata           |                      {}                        |
|     os-vol-host-attr:host    |                   devstack                     |
| os-vol-tenant-attr:tenant_id |       66265572db174a7aa66eba661f58eb9e          |
|             size             |                      8                         |
|         snapshot_id          |                     None                       |
|         source_volid         |                     None                       |
|            status            |                    in-use                      |
|     volume_image_metadata    |         {u'kernel_id': u'df430cc2...,          |
|                              |           u'image_id': u'397e713c...,          |
|                              |          u'ramdisk_id': u'3cf852bd...,         |
|                              |  u'image_name': u'cirros-0.3.2-x86_64-uec'}|   |
|         volume_type          |                     None                       |
+------------------------------+------------------------------------------------+
```

4.9.4   Resize a volume

1. To resize your volume, you must first detach it from the server. To detach the volume from your server, pass the server ID and volume ID to the following command:

```
$ nova volume-detach 84c6e57d-a6b1-44b6-81eb-fcb36afd31b5   573e024d-5235-49ce-8332-
be1576d323f8
```

The **volume-detach** command does not return any output.

2. List volumes:

```
$ cinder list
+----------------+-----------+-----------------+------+-------------+----------
+-------------+
|       ID       |  Status   |  Display Name   | Size | Volume Type | Bootable | Attached
 to |
+----------------+-----------+-----------------+------+-------------+----------
+-------------+
| 573e024d-52... | available |  my-new-volume  |  8   |    None     |   true   |
      |
| bd7cf584-45    | available | my-bootable-vol |  8   |    None     |   true   |
      |
+----------------+-----------+-----------------+------+-------------+----------
+-------------+
```

Note that the volume is now available.

3. Resize the volume by passing the volume ID and the new size (a value greater than the old one) as parameters:

```
$ cinder extend 573e024d-5235-49ce-8332-be1576d323f8 10
```

The **extend** command does not return any output.

4.9.5 Delete a volume

1. To delete your volume, you must first detach it from the server. To detach the volume from your server and check for the list of existing volumes, see steps 1 and 2 in *Section 4.9.4, "Resize a volume"*.

Delete the volume using either the volume name or ID:

```
$ cinder delete my-new-volume
```

The **delete** command does not return any output.

2. List the volumes again, and note that the status of your volume is `deleting`:

```
$ cinder list
+------------------+-----------+------------------+------+-------------+----------+
+-------------+
|       ID         |  Status   |  Display Name    | Size | Volume Type | Bootable |
Attached to |
+------------------+-----------+------------------+------+-------------+----------+
+-------------+
| 573e024d-523... | deleting  | my-new-volume    |  8   |    None     |   true   |
      |
| bd7cf584-45d... | available | my-bootable-vol  |  8   |    None     |   true   |
      |
+------------------+-----------+------------------+------+-------------+----------+
+-------------+
```

When the volume is fully deleted, it disappears from the list of volumes:

```
$ cinder list
+------------------+-----------+------------------+------+-------------+----------+
+-------------+
|       ID         |  Status   |  Display Name    | Size | Volume Type | Bootable |
Attached to |
+------------------+-----------+------------------+------+-------------+----------+
+-------------+
| bd7cf584-45d... | available | my-bootable-vol  |  8   |    None     |   true   |
      |
+------------------+-----------+------------------+------+-------------+----------+
+-------------+
```

4.9.6 Transfer a volume

You can transfer a volume from one owner to another by using the **`cinder transfer*`** commands. The volume donor, or original owner, creates a transfer request and sends the created transfer ID and authorization key to the volume recipient. The volume recipient, or new owner, accepts the transfer by using the ID and key.

 Note

The procedure for volume transfer is intended for tenants (both the volume donor and recipient) within the same cloud.

Use cases include:

- Create a custom bootable volume or a volume with a large data set and transfer it to a customer.

- For bulk import of data to the cloud, the data ingress system creates a new Block Storage volume, copies data from the physical device, and transfers device ownership to the end user.

4.9.6.1 Create a volume transfer request

1. While logged in as the volume donor, list the available volumes:

```
$ cinder list
+----------------+-----------+--------------+------+-------------+----------
-------------+
|       ID       |   Status  | Display Name | Size | Volume Type | Bootable | Attached
  to |
+----------------+-----------+--------------+------+-------------+----------
-------------+
| 72bfce9f-cac... |   error   |     None     |  1   |     None    |  false   |
    |
| a1cdace0-08e... | available |     None     |  1   |     None    |  false   |
    |
```

```
+---------------+-----------+---------------+-------+-------------+----------
+-------------+
```

2. As the volume donor, request a volume transfer authorization code for a specific volume:

```
$ cinder transfer-create volumeID
```

The volume must be in an `available` state or the request will be denied. If the transfer request is valid in the database (that is, it has not expired or been deleted), the volume is placed in an `awaiting transfer` state. For example:

```
$ cinder transfer-create a1cdace0-08e4-4dc7-b9dc-457e9bcfe25f
```

The output shows the volume transfer ID in the `id` row and the authorization key.

```
+-------------+------------------------------------------+
|  Property   |                 Value                    |
+-------------+------------------------------------------+
|  auth_key   |            b2c8e585cbc68a80              |
| created_at  |         2013-10-14T15:20:10.121458       |
|     id      |   6e4e9aa4-bed5-4f94-8f76-df43232f44dc   |
|    name     |                  None                    |
| volume_id   |   a1cdace0-08e4-4dc7-b9dc-457e9bcfe25f   |
+-------------+------------------------------------------+
```

 Note

Optionally, you can specify a name for the transfer by using the `--display-name displayName` parameter.

 Note

While the `auth_key` property is visible in the output of `cinder transfer-create VOLUME_ID`, it will not be available in subsequent `cinder transfer-show TRANSFER_ID` commands.

3. Send the volume transfer ID and authorization key to the new owner (for example, by email).

4. View pending transfers:

```
$ cinder transfer-list
+------------------------------------+------------------------------------+------+
|                 ID                 |              VolumeID              | Name |
+------------------------------------+------------------------------------+------+
| 6e4e9aa4-bed5-4f94-8f76-df43232f44dc | a1cdace0-08e4-4dc7-b9dc-457e9bcfe25f | None |
+------------------------------------+------------------------------------+------+
```

5. After the volume recipient, or new owner, accepts the transfer, you can see that the transfer is no longer available:

```
$ cinder transfer-list
+----+-----------+------+
| ID | Volume ID | Name |
+----+-----------+------+
+----+-----------+------+
```

4.9.6.2   Accept a volume transfer request

1. As the volume recipient, you must first obtain the transfer ID and authorization key from the original owner.

2. Accept the request:

```
$ cinder transfer-accept transferID authKey
```

For example:

```
$ cinder transfer-accept 6e4e9aa4-bed5-4f94-8f76-df43232f44dc
  b2c8e585cbc68a80
+-----------+------------------------------------+
|  Property |              Value                 |
+-----------+------------------------------------+
```

```
|     id     | 6e4e9aa4-bed5-4f94-8f76-df43232f44dc |
|    name    |                 None                 |
| volume_id  | a1cdace0-08e4-4dc7-b9dc-457e9bcfe25f |
+------------+--------------------------------------+
```

 Note

If you do not have a sufficient quota for the transfer, the transfer is refused.

4.9.6.3   Delete a volume transfer

1. List available volumes and their statuses:

```
$ cinder list
+-------------+-----------------+--------------+------+-------------+----------+-------------+
|     ID      |      Status     | Display Name | Size | Volume Type | Bootable | Attached to |
+-------------+-----------------+--------------+------+-------------+----------+-------------+
| 72bfce9f... |      error      |     None     |  1   |    None     |  false   |             |
| a1cdace0... |awaiting-transfer|     None     |  1   |    None     |  false   |             |
+-------------+-----------------+--------------+------+-------------+----------+-------------+
```

2. Find the matching transfer ID:

```
$ cinder transfer-list
+--------------------------------------+--------------------------------------+------+
|                  ID                  |               VolumeID               | Name |
+--------------------------------------+--------------------------------------+------+
| a6da6888-7cdf-4291-9c08-8c1f22426b8a | a1cdace0-08e4-4dc7-b9dc-457e9bcfe25f | None |
+--------------------------------------+--------------------------------------+------+
```

3. Delete the volume:

```
$ cinder transfer-delete transferID
```

For example:

```
$ cinder transfer-delete a6da6888-7cdf-4291-9c08-8c1f22426b8a
```

4. Verify that transfer list is now empty and that the volume is again available for transfer:

```
$ cinder transfer-list
+----+-----------+------+
| ID | Volume ID | Name |
+----+-----------+------+
+----+-----------+------+
```

```
$ cinder list
+-----------------+-----------+--------------+------+-------------+----------...
+-------------+
|       ID        |  Status   | Display Name | Size | Volume Type | Bootable | Attached
 to |
+-----------------+-----------+--------------+------+-------------+----------...
+-------------+
| 72bfce9f-ca... |   error   |     None     |  1   |    None     |  false   |
    |
| a1cdace0-08... | available |     None     |  1   |    None     |  false   |
    |
+-----------------+-----------+--------------+------+-------------+----------...
+-------------+
```

4.10 Manage shares

A share is provided by file storage. You can give access to a share to instances. To create and manage shares, you use manila client commands.

4.10.1 Migrate a share

As an administrator, you can migrate a share with its data from one location to another in a manner that is transparent to users and workloads.

Possible use cases for data migration include:

* Bring down a physical storage device for maintenance without disrupting workloads.

* Modify the properties of a share.

* Free up space in a thinly-provisioned back end.

Migrate a share with the **manila migrate** command, as shown in the following example:

```
$ manila migrate shareID destinationHost --force-host-copy True|False
```

In this example, `--force-host-copy True` forces the generic host-based migration mechanism and bypasses any driver optimizations. `destinationHost` is in this format `host#pool` which includes destination host and pool.

 Note

    If the user is not an administrator, the migration fails.

4.11 Manage flavors

In OpenStack, flavors define the compute, memory, and storage capacity of nova computing instances. To put it simply, a flavor is an available hardware configuration for a server. It defines the `size` of a virtual server that can be launched.

 Note

    Flavors can also determine on which compute host a flavor can be used to launch an instance. For information about customizing flavors, refer to the OpenStack Cloud Administrator Guide (http://docs.openstack.org/admin-guide-cloud/compute-flavors.html) ↗.

A flavor consists of the following parameters:

Flavor ID

Unique ID (integer or UUID) for the new flavor. If specifying 'auto', a UUID will be automatically generated.

Name

Name for the new flavor.

VCPUs

Number of virtual CPUs to use.

Memory MB

Amount of RAM to use (in megabytes).

Root Disk GB

Amount of disk space (in gigabytes) to use for the root (/) partition.

Ephemeral Disk GB

Amount of disk space (in gigabytes) to use for the ephemeral partition. If unspecified, the value is 0 by default. Ephemeral disks offer machine local disk storage linked to the lifecycle of a VM instance. When a VM is terminated, all data on the ephemeral disk is lost. Ephemeral disks are not included in any snapshots.

Swap

Amount of swap space (in megabytes) to use. If unspecified, the value is 0 by default.

The default flavors are:

Flavor	VCPUs	Disk (in GB)	RAM (in MB)
m1.tiny	1	1	512
m1.small	1	20	2048
m1.medium	2	40	4096
m1.large	4	80	8192
m1.xlarge	8	160	16384

You can create and manage flavors with the nova **flavor-*** commands provided by the `python-novaclient` package.

4.11.1 Create a flavor

1. List flavors to show the ID and name, the amount of memory, the amount of disk space for the root partition and for the ephemeral partition, the swap, and the number of virtual CPUs for each flavor:

```
$ nova flavor-list
```

2. To create a flavor, specify a name, ID, RAM size, disk size, and the number of VCPUs for the flavor, as follows:

```
$ nova flavor-create FLAVOR_NAME FLAVOR_ID RAM_IN_MB ROOT_DISK_IN_GB NUMBER_OF_VCPUS
```

 Note

Unique ID (integer or UUID) for the new flavor. If specifying 'auto', a UUID will be automatically generated.

Here is an example with additional optional parameters filled in that creates a public `extra tiny` flavor that automatically gets an ID assigned, with 256 MB memory, no disk space, and one VCPU. The rxtx-factor indicates the slice of bandwidth that the instances with this flavor can use (through the Virtual Interface (vif) creation in the hypervisor):

```
$ nova flavor-create --is-public true m1.extra_tiny auto 256 0 1 --rxtx-factor .1
```

3. If an individual user or group of users needs a custom flavor that you do not want other tenants to have access to, you can change the flavor's access to make it a private flavor. See Private Flavors in the OpenStack Operations Guide (http://docs.openstack.org/openstack-ops/content/private-flavors.html) .

For a list of optional parameters, run this command:

```
$ nova help flavor-create
```

4. After you create a flavor, assign it to a project by specifying the flavor name or ID and the tenant ID:

```
$ nova flavor-access-add FLAVOR TENANT_ID
```

5. In addition, you can set or unset `extra_spec` for the existing flavor. The `extra_spec` metadata keys can influence the instance directly when it is launched. If a flavor sets the `extra_spec key/value quota:vif_outbound_peak=65536`, the instance's out bound peak bandwidth I/O should be LTE 512 Mbps. There are several aspects that can work for an instance including `CPU limits`, `Disk tuning`, `Bandwidth I/O`, `Watchdog be-havior`, and `Random-number generator`. For information about supporting metadata keys, see the OpenStack Cloud Administrator Guide (http://docs.openstack.org/admin-guide-cloud/compute-flavors.html) ↗.

For a list of optional parameters, run this command:

```
$ nova help flavor-key
```

4.11.2 Delete a flavor

Delete a specified flavor, as follows:

```
$ nova flavor-delete FLAVOR_ID
```

4.12 Manage the OpenStack environment

This section includes tasks specific to the OpenStack environment.

4.12.1 Select hosts where instances are launched

With the appropriate permissions, you can select which host instances are launched on and which roles can boot instances on this host.

1. To select the host where instances are launched, use the `--availability_zone ZONE:HOST` parameter on the **nova boot** command.

For example:

```
$ nova boot --image <uuid> --flavor m1.tiny --key_name test --availability-zone
 nova:server2
```

2. To specify which roles can launch an instance on a specified host, enable the `create:forced_host` option in the `policy.json` file. By default, this option is enabled for only the admin role.

3. To view the list of valid compute hosts, use the **nova hypervisor-list** command.

```
$ nova hypervisor-list
+----+---------------------+
| ID | Hypervisor hostname |
+----+---------------------+
| 1  | server2             |
| 2  | server3             |
| 3  | server4             |
+----+---------------------+
```

4.12.2   Consider NUMA topology when booting instances

NUMA topology can exist on both the physical hardware of the host, and the virtual hardware of the instance. OpenStack Compute uses libvirt to tune instances to take advantage of NUMA topologies. The libvirt driver boot process looks at the NUMA topology field of both the instance and the host it is being booted on, and uses that information to generate an appropriate configuration.

If the host is NUMA capable, but the instance has not requested a NUMA topology, Compute attempts to pack the instance into a single cell. If this fails, though, Compute will not continue to try.

If the host is NUMA capable, and the instance has requested a specific NUMA topology, Compute will try to pin the vCPUs of different NUMA cells on the instance to the corresponding NUMA cells on the host. It will also expose the NUMA topology of the instance to the guest OS.

If you want Compute to pin a particular vCPU as part of this process, set the `vcpu_pin_set` parameter in the `nova.conf` configuration file. For more information about the `vcpu_pin_set` parameter, see the Configuration Reference Guide.

4.12.3 Evacuate instances

If a hardware malfunction or other error causes a cloud compute node to fail, you can evacuate instances to make them available again. You can optionally include the target host on the **evacuate** command. If you omit the host, the scheduler chooses the target host.

To preserve user data on the server disk, configure shared storage on the target host. When you evacuate the instance, Compute detects whether shared storage is available on the target host. Also, you must validate that the current VM host is not operational. Otherwise, the evacuation fails.

1. To find a host for the evacuated instance, list all hosts:

```
$ nova host-list
```

2. Evacuate the instance. You can use the `--password PWD` option to pass the instance password to the command. If you do not specify a password, the command generates and prints one after it finishes successfully. The following command evacuates a server from a failed host to HOST_B.

```
$ nova evacuate EVACUATED_SERVER_NAME HOST_B
```

The command rebuilds the instance from the original image or volume and returns a password. The command preserves the original configuration, which includes the instance ID, name, uid, IP address, and so on.

```
+-----------+--------------+
| Property  |    Value     |
+-----------+--------------+
| adminPass | kRAJpErnT4xZ |
+-----------+--------------+
```

3. To preserve the user disk data on the evacuated server, deploy Compute with a shared file system. To configure your system, see Configure migrations (http://docs.openstack.org/admin-guide-cloud/compute-configuring-migrations.html) ↗ in the `OpenStack Cloud Administrator Guide`. The following example does not change the password.

```
$ nova evacuate EVACUATED_SERVER_NAME HOST_B --on-shared-storage
```

4.12.4 Migrate single instance to another compute host

When you want to move an instance from one compute host to another, you can use the **nova migrate** command. The scheduler chooses the destination compute host based on its settings. This process does not assume that the instance has shared storage available on the target host.

1. To list the VMs you want to migrate, run:

   ```
   $ nova list
   ```

2. After selecting a VM from the list, run this command where *VM_ID* is set to the ID in the list returned in the previous step:

   ```
   $ nova show VM_ID
   ```

3. Now, use the **nova migrate** command.

   ```
   $ nova migrate VM_ID
   ```

4. To migrate an instance and watch the status, use this example script:

   ```
   #!/bin/bash

   # Provide usage
   usage() {
   echo "Usage: $0 VM_ID"
   exit 1
   }

   [[ $# -eq 0 ]] && usage

   # Migrate the VM to an alternate hypervisor
   echo -n "Migrating instance to alternate host"
   VM_ID=$1
   nova migrate $VM_ID
   VM_OUTPUT=`nova show $VM_ID`
   VM_STATUS=`echo "$VM_OUTPUT" | grep status | awk '{print $4}'`
   ```

```
while [[ "$VM_STATUS" != "VERIFY_RESIZE" ]]; do
echo -n "."
sleep 2
VM_OUTPUT=`nova show $VM_ID`
VM_STATUS=`echo "$VM_OUTPUT" | grep status | awk '{print $4}'`
done
nova resize-confirm $VM_ID
echo " instance migrated and resized."
echo;

# Show the details for the VM
echo "Updated instance details:"
nova show $VM_ID

# Pause to allow users to examine VM details
read -p "Pausing, press <enter> to exit."
```

 Note

If you see this error, it means you are either trying the command with the wrong credentials, such as a non-admin user, or the `policy.json` file prevents migration for your user:

```
ERROR            (Forbidden):         Policy          doesn't         allow
compute_extension:admin_actions:migrate to be performed. (HTTP 403)
```

The instance is booted from a new host, but preserves its configuration including its ID, name, any metadata, IP address, and other properties.

4.12.5 Manage IP addresses

Each instance has a private, fixed IP address (assigned when launched) and can also have a public, or floating, address. Private IP addresses are used for communication between instances, and public addresses are used for communication with networks outside the cloud, including the Internet.

- By default, both administrative and end users can associate floating IP addresses with projects and instances. You can change user permissions for managing IP addresses by updating the `/etc/nova/policy.json` file. For basic floating-IP procedures, refer to the Manage IP Addresses section in the OpenStack End User Guide (http://docs.openstack.org/user-guide/) ↗.

- For details on creating public networks using OpenStack Networking (`neutron`), refer to the OpenStack Cloud Administrator Guide (http://docs.openstack.org/admin-guide-cloud/networking_adv-features.html) ↗. No floating IP addresses are created by default in OpenStack Networking.

As an administrator using legacy networking (`nova-network`), you can use the following bulk commands to list, create, and delete ranges of floating IP addresses. These addresses can then be associated with instances by end users.

4.12.5.1 List addresses for all projects

To list all floating IP addresses for all projects, run:

```
$ nova floating-ip-bulk-list
+------------+---------------+---------------+--------+-----------+
| project_id | address       | instance_uuid | pool   | interface |
+------------+---------------+---------------+--------+-----------+
| None       | 172.24.4.225  | None          | public | eth0      |
| None       | 172.24.4.226  | None          | public | eth0      |
| None       | 172.24.4.227  | None          | public | eth0      |
| None       | 172.24.4.228  | None          | public | eth0      |
| None       | 172.24.4.229  | None          | public | eth0      |
| None       | 172.24.4.230  | None          | public | eth0      |
| None       | 172.24.4.231  | None          | public | eth0      |
| None       | 172.24.4.232  | None          | public | eth0      |
| None       | 172.24.4.233  | None          | public | eth0      |
| None       | 172.24.4.234  | None          | public | eth0      |
| None       | 172.24.4.235  | None          | public | eth0      |
| None       | 172.24.4.236  | None          | public | eth0      |
| None       | 172.24.4.237  | None          | public | eth0      |
| None       | 172.24.4.238  | None          | public | eth0      |
```

```
| None        | 192.168.253.1 | None          | test   | eth0      |
| None        | 192.168.253.2 | None          | test   | eth0      |
| None        | 192.168.253.3 | None          | test   | eth0      |
| None        | 192.168.253.4 | None          | test   | eth0      |
| None        | 192.168.253.5 | None          | test   | eth0      |
| None        | 192.168.253.6 | None          | test   | eth0      |
+-----------+-------------+---------------+-------+----------+
```

4.12.5.2 Bulk create floating IP addresses

To create a range of floating IP addresses, run:

```
$ nova floating-ip-bulk-create [--pool POOL_NAME] [--interface INTERFACE] RANGE_TO_CREATE
```

For example:

```
$ nova floating-ip-bulk-create --pool test 192.168.1.56/29
```

By default, floating-ip-bulk-create uses the public pool and eth0 interface values.

 Note

You should use a range of free IP addresses that is correct for your network. If you are not sure, at least try to avoid the DHCP address range:

- Pick a small range (/29 gives an 8 address range, 6 of which will be usable).

- Use **nmap** to check a range's availability. For example, 192.168.1.56/29 represents a small range of addresses (192.168.1.56-63, with 57-62 usable), and you could run the command **nmap -sn 192.168.1.56/29** to check whether the entire range is currently unused.

4.12.5.3 Bulk delete floating IP addresses

To delete a range of floating IP addresses, run:

```
$ nova floating-ip-bulk-delete RANGE_TO_DELETE
```

For example:

```
$ nova floating-ip-bulk-delete 192.168.1.56/29
```

4.12.6   Launch and manage stacks using the CLI

The Orchestration service provides a template-based orchestration engine for the OpenStack cloud, which can be used to create and manage cloud infrastructure resources such as storage, networking, instances, and applications as a repeatable running environment.

Templates are used to create stacks, which are collections of resources. For example, a stack might include instances, floating IPs, volumes, security groups, or users. The Orchestration service offers access to all OpenStack core services via a single modular template, with additional orchestration capabilities such as auto-scaling and basic high availability.

For information about:

* basic creation and deletion of Orchestration stacks, refer to the OpenStack End User Guide (http://docs.openstack.org/user-guide/dashboard_stacks.html) ↗

* **heat** CLI commands, see the OpenStack Command Line Interface Reference (http://docs.openstack.org/cli-reference/heat.html) ↗

As an administrator, you can also carry out stack functions on behalf of your users. For example, to resume, suspend, or delete a stack, run:

```
$ heat action-resume stackID
$ heat action-suspend stackID
$ heat stack-delete stackID
```

4.12.7   Show usage statistics for hosts and instances

You can show basic statistics on resource usage for hosts and instances.

Note

For more sophisticated monitoring, see the ceilometer (https://launchpad.net/ceilometer) ↗ project. You can also use tools, such as Ganglia (http://ganglia.info/) ↗ or Graphite (http://graphite.wikidot.com/) ↗, to gather more detailed data.

4.12.7.1   Show host usage statistics

The following examples show the host usage statistics for a host called `devstack`.

- List the hosts and the nova-related services that run on them:

```
$ nova host-list
+-----------+-------------+----------+
| host_name | service     | zone     |
+-----------+-------------+----------+
| devstack  | conductor   | internal |
| devstack  | compute     | nova     |
| devstack  | cert        | internal |
| devstack  | network     | internal |
| devstack  | scheduler   | internal |
| devstack  | consoleauth | internal |
+-----------+-------------+----------+
```

- Get a summary of resource usage of all of the instances running on the host:

```
$ nova host-describe devstack
+----------+----------------------------------+-----+-----------+---------+
| HOST     | PROJECT                          | cpu | memory_mb | disk_gb |
+----------+----------------------------------+-----+-----------+---------+
| devstack | (total)                          | 2   | 4003      | 157     |
| devstack | (used_now)                       | 3   | 5120      | 40      |
| devstack | (used_max)                       | 3   | 4608      | 40      |
| devstack | b70d90d65e464582b6b2161cf3603ced | 1   | 512       | 0       |
| devstack | 66265572db174a7aa66eba661f58eb9e | 2   | 4096      | 40      |
+----------+----------------------------------+-----+-----------+---------+
```

The `cpu` column shows the sum of the virtual CPUs for instances running on the host.

The `memory_mb` column shows the sum of the memory (in MB) allocated to the instances that run on the host.

The `disk_gb` column shows the sum of the root and ephemeral disk sizes (in GB) of the instances that run on the host.

The row that has the value `used_now` in the `PROJECT` column shows the sum of the resources allocated to the instances that run on the host, plus the resources allocated to the virtual machine of the host itself.

The row that has the value `used_max` in the `PROJECT` column shows the sum of the resources allocated to the instances that run on the host.

 Note

> These values are computed by using information about the flavors of the instances that run on the hosts. This command does not query the CPU usage, memory usage, or hard disk usage of the physical host.

4.12.7.2 Show instance usage statistics

- Get CPU, memory, I/O, and network statistics for an instance.

  - List instances:

```
$ nova list
+----------+----------------------+--------+------------+-------------+-------------
+------------------+
| ID       | Name                 | Status | Task State | Power State | Networks
    |
+----------+----------------------+--------+------------+-------------+-------------
+------------------+
| 84c6e... | myCirrosServer       | ACTIVE | None       | Running     |
 private=10.0.0.3 |
| 8a995... | myInstanceFromVolume | ACTIVE | None       | Running     |
 private=10.0.0.4 |
```

```
+----------+-------------------+--------+-----------+-------------
+-----------------+
```

• Get diagnostic statistics:

```
$ nova diagnostics myCirrosServer
+-----------------+----------------+
| Property        | Value          |
+-----------------+----------------+
| vnet1_rx        | 1210744        |
| cpu0_time       | 19624610000000 |
| vda_read        | 0              |
| vda_write       | 0              |
| vda_write_req   | 0              |
| vnet1_tx        | 863734         |
| vnet1_tx_errors | 0              |
| vnet1_rx_drop   | 0              |
| vnet1_tx_packets| 3855           |
| vnet1_tx_drop   | 0              |
| vnet1_rx_errors | 0              |
| memory          | 2097152        |
| vnet1_rx_packets| 5485           |
| vda_read_req    | 0              |
| vda_errors      | -1             |
+-----------------+----------------+
```

• Get summary statistics for each tenant:

```
$ nova usage-list
Usage from 2013-06-25 to 2013-07-24:
+----------------------------------+-----------+--------------+-----------
+---------------+
| Tenant ID                        | Instances | RAM MB-Hours | CPU Hours | Disk GB-Hours
  |
+----------------------------------+-----------+--------------+-----------
+---------------+
```

```
| b70d90d65e464582b6b2161cf3603ced | 1          | 344064.44    | 672.00    | 0.00
|

| 66265572db174a7aa66eba661f58eb9e | 3          | 671626.76    | 327.94    | 6558.86
|

+-------------------------------------------+------------+---------------+----------
+---------------+
```

4.13 Manage quotas

To prevent system capacities from being exhausted without notification, you can set up quotas. Quotas are operational limits. For example, the number of gigabytes allowed for each tenant can be controlled so that cloud resources are optimized. Quotas can be enforced at both the tenant (or project) and the tenant-user level.

Using the command-line interface, you can manage quotas for the OpenStack Compute service, the OpenStack Block Storage service, and the OpenStack Networking service.

The cloud operator typically changes default values because a tenant requires more than ten volumes or 1 TB on a compute node.

 Note

To view all tenants (projects), run:

```
$ openstack project list
+------------------------------------+----------+
| ID                                 | Name     |
+------------------------------------+----------+
| e66d97ac1b704897853412fc8450f7b9   | admin    |
| bf4a37b885fe46bd86e999e50adad1d3   | services |
| 21bd1c7c95234fd28f589b60903606fa   | tenant01 |
| f599c5cd1cba4125ae3d7caed08e288c   | tenant02 |
+------------------------------------+----------+
```

To display all current users for a tenant, run:

```
$ openstack user list --project PROJECT_NAME
+------------------------------------+--------+
```

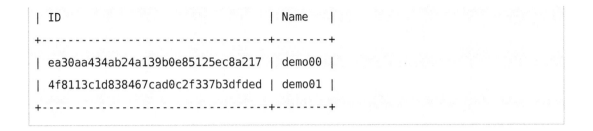

```
| ID                               | Name   |
+----------------------------------+--------+
| ea30aa434ab24a139b0e85125ec8a217 | demo00 |
| 4f8113c1d838467cad0c2f337b3dfded | demo01 |
+----------------------------------+--------+
```

4.13.1   Manage Compute service quotas

As an administrative user, you can use the **nova quota-*** commands, which are provided by the `python-novaclient` package, to update the Compute service quotas for a specific tenant or tenant user, as well as update the quota defaults for a new tenant.

Compute quota descriptions

TABLE 4.4: COMPUTE QUOTA DESCRIPTIONS

Quota name	Description
cores	Number of instance cores (VCPUs) allowed per tenant.
fixed-ips	Number of fixed IP addresses allowed per tenant. This number must be equal to or greater than the number of allowed instances.
floating-ips	Number of floating IP addresses allowed per tenant.
injected-file-content-bytes	Number of content bytes allowed per injected file.
injected-file-path-bytes	Length of injected file path.
injected-files	Number of injected files allowed per tenant.
instances	Number of instances allowed per tenant.
key-pairs	Number of key pairs allowed per user.
metadata-items	Number of metadata items allowed per instance.

Quota name	Description
ram	Megabytes of instance ram allowed per tenant.
security-groups	Number of security groups per tenant.
security-group-rules	Number of rules per security group.

4.13.1.1 View and update Compute quotas for a tenant (project)

4.13.1.1.1 To view and update default quota values

1. List all default quotas for all tenants:

```
$ nova quota-defaults
```

For example:

```
$ nova quota-defaults
+-----------------------------+-------+
| Quota                       | Limit |
+-----------------------------+-------+
| instances                   | 10    |
| cores                       | 20    |
| ram                         | 51200 |
| floating_ips                | 10    |
| fixed_ips                   | -1    |
| metadata_items              | 128   |
| injected_files              | 5     |
| injected_file_content_bytes | 10240 |
| injected_file_path_bytes    | 255   |
| key_pairs                   | 100   |
| security_groups             | 10    |
| security_group_rules        | 20    |
```

```
+-----------------------------+-------+
```

2. Update a default value for a new tenant.

```
$ nova quota-class-update --KEY VALUE default
```

For example:

```
$ nova quota-class-update --instances 15 default
```

4.13.1.1.2   To view quota values for an existing tenant (project)

1. Place the tenant ID in a usable variable.

```
$ tenant=$(openstack project show -f value -c id TENANT_NAME)
```

2. List the currently set quota values for a tenant.

```
$ nova quota-show --tenant $tenant
```

For example:

```
$ nova quota-show --tenant $tenant
+-----------------------------+-------+
| Quota                       | Limit |
+-----------------------------+-------+
| instances                   | 10    |
| cores                       | 20    |
| ram                         | 51200 |
| floating_ips                | 10    |
| fixed_ips                   | -1    |
| metadata_items              | 128   |
| injected_files              | 5     |
| injected_file_content_bytes | 10240 |
| injected_file_path_bytes    | 255   |
| key_pairs                   | 100   |
| security_groups             | 10    |
```

```
| security_group_rules      | 20   |
+---------------------------+------+
```

4.13.1.1.3   To update quota values for an existing tenant (project)

1. Obtain the tenant ID.

```
$ tenant=$(openstack project show -f value -c id TENANT_NAME)
```

2. Update a particular quota value.

```
$ nova quota-update --QUOTA_NAME QUOTA_VALUE TENANT_ID
```

For example:

```
$ nova quota-update --floating-ips 20 $tenant
$ nova quota-show --tenant $tenant
+-----------------------------+-------+
| Quota                       | Limit |
+-----------------------------+-------+
| instances                   | 10    |
| cores                       | 20    |
| ram                         | 51200 |
| floating_ips                | 20    |
| fixed_ips                   | -1    |
| metadata_items              | 128   |
| injected_files              | 5     |
| injected_file_content_bytes | 10240 |
| injected_file_path_bytes    | 255   |
| key_pairs                   | 100   |
| security_groups             | 10    |
| security_group_rules        | 20    |
+-----------------------------+-------+
```

Note

To view a list of options for the **quota-update** command, run:

```
$ nova help quota-update
```

4.13.1.2 View and update Compute quotas for a tenant user

4.13.1.2.1 To view quota values for a tenant user

1. Place the user ID in a usable variable.

```
$ tenantUser=$(openstack user show -f value -c id USER_NAME)
```

2. Place the user's tenant ID in a usable variable, as follows:

```
$ tenant=$(openstack project show -f value -c id TENANT_NAME)
```

3. List the currently set quota values for a tenant user.

```
$ nova quota-show --user $tenantUser --tenant $tenant
```

For example:

```
$ nova quota-show --user $tenantUser --tenant $tenant
+-----------------------------+-------+
| Quota                       | Limit |
+-----------------------------+-------+
| instances                   | 10    |
| cores                       | 20    |
| ram                         | 51200 |
| floating_ips                | 20    |
| fixed_ips                   | -1    |
| metadata_items              | 128   |
```

```
| injected_files              | 5     |
| injected_file_content_bytes | 10240 |
| injected_file_path_bytes    | 255   |
| key_pairs                   | 100   |
| security_groups             | 10    |
| security_group_rules        | 20    |
+-----------------------------+-------+
```

4.13.1.2.2 To update quota values for a tenant user

1. Place the user ID in a usable variable.

```
$ tenantUser=$(openstack user show -f value -c id USER_NAME)
```

2. Place the user's tenant ID in a usable variable, as follows:

```
$ tenant=$(openstack project show -f value -c id TENANT_NAME)
```

3. Update a particular quota value, as follows:

```
$ nova quota-update  --user $tenantUser --QUOTA_NAME QUOTA_VALUE $tenant
```

For example:

```
$ nova quota-update --user $tenantUser --floating-ips 12 $tenant
$ nova quota-show --user $tenantUser --tenant $tenant
+-----------------------------+-------+
| Quota                       | Limit |
+-----------------------------+-------+
| instances                   | 10    |
| cores                       | 20    |
| ram                         | 51200 |
| floating_ips                | 12    |
| fixed_ips                   | -1    |
| metadata_items              | 128   |
| injected_files              | 5     |
```

```
| injected_file_content_bytes | 10240 |
| injected_file_path_bytes    | 255   |
| key_pairs                   | 100   |
| security_groups             | 10    |
| security_group_rules        | 20    |
+-----------------------------+-------+
```

 Note

To view a list of options for the **quota-update** command, run:

```
$ nova help quota-update
```

4.13.1.2.3   To display the current quota usage for a tenant user

Use **nova absolute-limits** to get a list of the current quota values and the current quota usage:

```
$ nova absolute-limits --tenant TENANT_NAME
+------------------------+-------+
| Name                   | Value |
+------------------------+-------+
| maxServerMeta          | 128   |
| maxPersonality         | 5     |
| maxImageMeta           | 128   |
| maxPersonalitySize     | 10240 |
| maxTotalRAMSize        | 51200 |
| maxSecurityGroupRules  | 20    |
| maxTotalKeypairs       | 100   |
| totalRAMUsed           | 0     |
| maxSecurityGroups      | 10    |
| totalFloatingIpsUsed   | 0     |
| totalInstancesUsed     | 0     |
| totalSecurityGroupsUsed | 0    |
| maxTotalFloatingIps    | 10    |
```

```
| maxTotalInstances      | 10    |
| totalCoresUsed         | 0     |
| maxTotalCores          | 20    |
+------------------------+-------+
```

4.13.2   Manage Block Storage service quotas

As an administrative user, you can update the OpenStack Block Storage service quotas for a project. You can also update the quota defaults for a new project.

Block Storage quotas

TABLE 4.5: BLOCK STORAGE QUOTAS

Property name	Defines the number of
gigabytes	Volume gigabytes allowed for each project.
snapshots	Volume snapshots allowed for each project.
volumes	Volumes allowed for each project.

4.13.2.1   View Block Storage quotas

Administrative users can view Block Storage service quotas.

1. Obtain the project ID.

   For example:

   ```
   $ project_id=$(openstack project show -f value -c id PROJECT_NAME)
   ```

2. List the default quotas for a project (tenant):

   ```
   $ cinder quota-defaults PROJECT_ID
   ```

   For example:

   ```
   $ cinder quota-defaults $project_id
   ```

```
+-----------+-------+
|  Property | Value |
+-----------+-------+
| gigabytes |  1000 |
| snapshots |   10  |
|  volumes  |   10  |
+-----------+-------+
```

3. View Block Storage service quotas for a project (tenant):

```
$ cinder quota-show PROJECT_ID
```

For example:

```
$ cinder quota-show $project_id
+-----------+-------+
|  Property | Value |
+-----------+-------+
| gigabytes |  1000 |
| snapshots |   10  |
|  volumes  |   10  |
+-----------+-------+
```

4. Show the current usage of a per-project quota:

```
$ cinder quota-usage PROJECT_ID
```

For example:

```
$ cinder quota-usage $project_id
+-----------+--------+----------+-------+
|    Type   | In_use | Reserved | Limit |
+-----------+--------+----------+-------+
| gigabytes |    0   |    0     |  1000 |
| snapshots |    0   |    0     |   10  |
|  volumes  |    0   |    0     |   15  |
+-----------+--------+----------+-------+
```

4.13.2.2 Edit and update Block Storage service quotas

Administrative users can edit and update Block Storage service quotas.

1. Clear per-project quota limits.

```
$ cinder quota-delete PROJECT_ID
```

2. To update a default value for a new project, update the property in the *cinder.quota* section of the `/etc/cinder/cinder.conf` file. For more information, see the Block Storage Configuration Reference (http://docs.openstack.org/liberty/config-reference/content/ch_configuring-openstack-block-storage.html) ↗ .

3. To update Block Storage service quotas for an existing project (tenant)

```
$ cinder quota-update --QUOTA_NAME QUOTA_VALUE PROJECT_ID
```

Replace QUOTA_NAME with the quota that is to be updated; NEW_VALUE with the required new value and PROJECT_ID with required project ID
For example:

```
$ cinder quota-update --volumes 15 $project_id
$ cinder quota-show $project_id
+-----------+-------+
| Property  | Value |
+-----------+-------+
| gigabytes |  1000 |
| snapshots |    10 |
|  volumes  |    15 |
+-----------+-------+
```

4. Clear per-project quota limits.

```
$ cinder quota-delete PROJECT_ID
```

4.13.2.3 Remove a service

1. Determine the binary and host of the service you want to remove.

```
$ cinder service-list
+------------------+-------------------+------+---------+-------
+-----------------------------+----------------+
|     Binary       |       Host        | Zone | Status | State |     Updated_at
       | Disabled Reason |
+------------------+-------------------+------+---------+-------
+-----------------------------+----------------+
| cinder-scheduler |       devstack    | nova | enabled |  up  |
 2015-10-13T15:21:48.000000 |      -         |
| cinder-volume    | devstack@lvmdriver-1 | nova | enabled |  up  |
 2015-10-13T15:21:52.000000 |      -         |
+------------------+-------------------+------+---------+-------
+-----------------------------+----------------+
```

2. Disable the service.

```
$ cinder service-disable HOST_NAME BINARY_NAME
```

3. Remove the service from the database.

```
$ cinder-manage service remove BINARY_NAME HOST_NAME
```

4.13.3   Manage Networking service quotas

A quota limits the number of available resources. A default quota might be enforced for all tenants. When you try to create more resources than the quota allows, an error occurs:

```
$ neutron net-create test_net
 Quota exceeded for resources: ['network']
```

Per-tenant quota configuration is also supported by the quota extension API. See *Section 4.13.3.2, "Configure per-tenant quotas"* for details.

4.13.3.1 Basic quota configuration

In the Networking default quota mechanism, all tenants have the same quota values, such as the number of resources that a tenant can create.

The quota value is defined in the OpenStack Networking `neutron.conf` configuration file. To disable quotas for a specific resource, such as network, subnet, or port, remove a corresponding item from `quota_items`. This example shows the default quota values:

```
[quotas]
# resource name(s) that are supported in quota features
quota_items = network,subnet,port


# number of networks allowed per tenant, and minus means unlimited
quota_network = 10


# number of subnets allowed per tenant, and minus means unlimited
quota_subnet = 10


# number of ports allowed per tenant, and minus means unlimited
quota_port = 50


# default driver to use for quota checks
quota_driver = neutron.quota.ConfDriver
```

OpenStack Networking also supports quotas for L3 resources: router and floating IP. Add these lines to the `quotas` section in the `neutron.conf` file:

```
[quotas]
# number of routers allowed per tenant, and minus means unlimited
quota_router = 10


# number of floating IPs allowed per tenant, and minus means unlimited
quota_floatingip = 50
```

 Note

The `quota_items` option does not affect these quotas.

OpenStack Networking also supports quotas for security group resources: number of security groups and the number of rules for each security group. Add these lines to the `quotas` section in the `neutron.conf` file:

```
[quotas]
# number of security groups per tenant, and minus means unlimited
quota_security_group = 10

# number of security rules allowed per tenant, and minus means unlimited
quota_security_group_rule = 100
```

 Note

The `quota_items` option does not affect these quotas.

4.13.3.2   Configure per-tenant quotas

OpenStack Networking also supports per-tenant quota limit by quota extension API.

Use these commands to manage per-tenant quotas:

neutron quota-delete
Delete defined quotas for a specified tenant

neutron quota-list
Lists defined quotas for all tenants

neutron quota-show
Shows quotas for a specified tenant

neutron quota-update
Updates quotas for a specified tenant

Only users with the `admin` role can change a quota value. By default, the default set of quotas are enforced for all tenants, so no **quota-create** command exists.

1. Configure Networking to show per-tenant quotas
   Set the `quota_driver` option in the `neutron.conf` file.

```
quota_driver = neutron.db.quota_db.DbQuotaDriver
```

When you set this option, the output for Networking commands shows `quotas`.

2. List Networking extensions.

   To list the Networking extensions, run this command:

   ```
   $ neutron ext-list -c alias -c name
   ```

   The command shows the `quotas` extension, which provides per-tenant quota management support.

   ```
   +-----------------+---------------------------+
   | alias           | name                      |
   +-----------------+---------------------------+
   | agent_scheduler | Agent Schedulers          |
   | security-group  | security-group            |
   | binding         | Port Binding              |
   | quotas          | Quota management support  |
   | agent           | agent                     |
   | provider        | Provider Network          |
   | router          | Neutron L3 Router         |
   | lbaas           | LoadBalancing service     |
   | extraroute      | Neutron Extra Route       |
   +-----------------+---------------------------+
   ```

3. Show information for the quotas extension.

   To show information for the `quotas` extension, run this command:

   ```
   $ neutron ext-show quotas
   +-------------+-------------------------------------------------------+
   | Field       | Value                                                 |
   +-------------+-------------------------------------------------------+
   | alias       | quotas                                                |
   | description | Expose functions for quotas management per tenant     |
   | links       |                                                       |
   | name        | Quota management support                              |
   ```

```
| namespace   | http://docs.openstack.org/network/ext/quotas-sets/api/v2.0 |
| updated     | 2012-07-29T10:00:00-00:00                                  |
+-------------+------------------------------------------------------------+
```

 Note

Only some plug-ins support per-tenant quotas. Specifically, Open vSwitch, Linux Bridge, and VMware NSX support them, but new versions of other plug-ins might bring additional functionality. See the documentation for each plug-in.

4. List tenants who have per-tenant quota support.

The **quota-list** command lists tenants for which the per-tenant quota is enabled. The command does not list tenants with default quota support. You must be an administrative user to run this command:

```
$ neutron quota-list
+------------+---------+------+--------+--------+----------------------------------+
| floatingip | network | port | router | subnet | tenant_id                        |
+------------+---------+------+--------+--------+----------------------------------+
|         20 |       5 |   20 |     10 |      5 | 6f88036c45344d9999a1f971e4882723 |
|         25 |      10 |   30 |     10 |     10 | bff5c9455ee24231b5bc713c1b96d422 |
+------------+---------+------+--------+--------+----------------------------------+
```

5. Show per-tenant quota values.

The **quota-show** command reports the current set of quota limits for the specified tenant. Non-administrative users can run this command without the --tenant_id parameter. If per-tenant quota limits are not enabled for the tenant, the command shows the default set of quotas.

```
$ neutron quota-show --tenant_id 6f88036c45344d9999a1f971e4882723
+------------+-------+
| Field      | Value |
+------------+-------+
| floatingip | 20    |
| network    | 5     |
| port       | 20    |
| router     | 10    |
```

```
| subnet      | 5     |
+-------------+-------+
```

The following command shows the command output for a non-administrative user.

```
$ neutron quota-show
+-------------+-------+
| Field       | Value |
+-------------+-------+
| floatingip  | 20    |
| network     | 5     |
| port        | 20    |
| router      | 10    |
| subnet      | 5     |
+-------------+-------+
```

6. Update quota values for a specified tenant.

   Use the **quota-update** command to update a quota for a specified tenant.

```
$ neutron quota-update --tenant_id 6f88036c45344d9999a1f971e4882723 --network 5
+-------------+-------+
| Field       | Value |
+-------------+-------+
| floatingip  | 50    |
| network     | 5     |
| port        | 50    |
| router      | 10    |
| subnet      | 10    |
+-------------+-------+
```

You can update quotas for multiple resources through one command.

```
$ neutron quota-update --tenant_id 6f88036c45344d9999a1f971e4882723 --subnet 5 --port 20
+-------------+-------+
| Field       | Value |
+-------------+-------+
| floatingip  | 50    |
```

```
| network  | 5   |
| port     | 20  |
| router   | 10  |
| subnet   | 5   |
+----------+-----+
```

To update the limits for an L3 resource such as, router or floating IP, you must define new values for the quotas after the `--` directive.

This example updates the limit of the number of floating IPs for the specified tenant.

```
$ neutron quota-update --tenant_id 6f88036c45344d9999a1f971e4882723 -- --floatingip 20
+------------+-------+
| Field      | Value |
+------------+-------+
| floatingip | 20    |
| network    | 5     |
| port       | 20    |
| router     | 10    |
| subnet     | 5     |
+------------+-------+
```

You can update the limits of multiple resources by including L2 resources and L3 resource through one command:

```
$ neutron quota-update --tenant_id 6f88036c45344d9999a1f971e4882723 --network 3 --subnet
 3 --port 3 -- --floatingip 3 --router 3
+------------+-------+
| Field      | Value |
+------------+-------+
| floatingip | 3     |
| network    | 3     |
| port       | 3     |
| router     | 3     |
| subnet     | 3     |
+------------+-------+
```

7. Delete per-tenant quota values.

To clear per-tenant quota limits, use the **quota-delete** command.

```
$ neutron quota-delete --tenant_id 6f88036c45344d9999a1f971e4882723
  Deleted quota: 6f88036c45344d9999a1f971e4882723
```

After you run this command, you can see that quota values for the tenant are reset to the default values.

```
$ neutron quota-show --tenant_id 6f88036c45344d9999a1f971e4882723
+------------+-------+
| Field      | Value |
+------------+-------+
| floatingip | 50    |
| network    | 10    |
| port       | 50    |
| router     | 10    |
| subnet     | 10    |
+------------+-------+
```

4.14 Analyze log files

Use the swift command-line client to analyze log files.

The swift client is simple to use, scalable, and flexible.

Use the swift client `-o` or `-output` option to get short answers to questions about logs.

You can use the `-o` or `--output` option with a single object download to redirect the command output to a specific file or to STDOUT (-). The ability to redirect the output to STDOUT enables you to pipe (|) data without saving it to disk first.

4.14.1 Upload and analyze log files

1. This example assumes that `logtest` directory contains the following log files.

```
2010-11-16-21_access.log
2010-11-16-22_access.log
```

```
2010-11-15-21_access.log
2010-11-15-22_access.log
```

Each file uses the following line format.

```
Nov 15 21:53:52 lucid64 proxy-server - 127.0.0.1 15/Nov/2010/22/53/52 DELETE /v1/
AUTH_cd4f57824deb4248a533f2c28bf156d3/2eefc05599d44df38a7f18b0b42ffedd HTTP/1.0 204 - \
 - test%3Atester%2CAUTH_tkcdab3c6296e249d7b7e2454ee57266ff - - - txaba5984c-aac7-460e-
b04b-afc43f0c6571 - 0.0432
```

2. Change into the `logtest` directory.

```
$ cd logtest
```

3. Upload the log files into the `logtest` container.

```
$ swift -A http://swift-auth.com:11000/v1.0 -U test:tester -K testing upload logtest
 *.log
```

```
2010-11-16-21_access.log
2010-11-16-22_access.log
2010-11-15-21_access.log
2010-11-15-22_access.log
```

4. Get statistics for the account.

```
$ swift -A http://swift-auth.com:11000/v1.0 -U test:tester -K testing \
-q stat
```

```
Account: AUTH_cd4f57824deb4248a533f2c28bf156d3
Containers: 1
Objects: 4
Bytes: 5888268
```

5. Get statistics for the `logtest` container.

```
$ swift -A http://swift-auth.com:11000/v1.0 -U test:tester -K testing \
stat logtest
```

```
Account: AUTH_cd4f57824deb4248a533f2c28bf156d3
Container: logtest
Objects: 4
Bytes: 5864468
Read ACL:
Write ACL:
```

6. List all objects in the logtest container.

```
$ swift -A http:///swift-auth.com:11000/v1.0 -U test:tester -K testing \
list logtest
```

```
2010-11-15-21_access.log
2010-11-15-22_access.log
2010-11-16-21_access.log
2010-11-16-22_access.log
```

4.14.2 Download and analyze an object

This example uses the `-o` option and a hyphen (-) to get information about an object.

Use the **swift download** command to download the object. On this command, stream the output to `awk` to break down requests by return code and the date `2200 on November 16th, 2010`.

Using the log line format, find the request type in column 9 and the return code in column 12.

After `awk` processes the output, it pipes it to `sort` and `uniq -c` to sum up the number of occurrences for each request type and return code combination.

1. Download an object.

```
$ swift -A http://swift-auth.com:11000/v1.0 -U test:tester -K testing \
    download -o - logtest 2010-11-16-22_access.log | awk '{ print \
    $9"-"$12}' | sort | uniq -c
```

```
805 DELETE-204
```

```
12 DELETE-404

2 DELETE-409

723 GET-200

142 GET-204

74 GET-206

80 GET-304

34 GET-401

5 GET-403

18 GET-404

166 GET-412

2 GET-416

50 HEAD-200

17 HEAD-204

20 HEAD-401

8 HEAD-404

30 POST-202

25 POST-204

22 POST-400

6 POST-404

842 PUT-201

2 PUT-202

32 PUT-400

4 PUT-403

4 PUT-404

2 PUT-411

6 PUT-412

6 PUT-413

2 PUT-422

8 PUT-499
```

2. Discover how many PUT requests are in each log file.

   Use a bash for loop with awk and swift with the `-o` or `--output` option and a hyphen
   (`-`) to discover how many PUT requests are in each log file.

   Run the **swift list** command to list objects in the logtest container. Then, for each item
   in the list, run the **swift download -o -** command. Pipe the output into grep to filter
   the PUT requests. Finally, pipe into `wc -l` to count the lines.

```
$ for f in `swift -A http://swift-auth.com:11000/v1.0 -U test:tester \
 -K testing list logtest` ; \
        do  echo -ne "PUTS - " ; swift -A \
        http://swift-auth.com:11000/v1.0 -U test:tester \
        -K testing download -o -  logtest $f | grep PUT | wc -l ; \
    done
```

```
2010-11-15-21_access.log - PUTS - 402
2010-11-15-22_access.log - PUTS - 1091
2010-11-16-21_access.log - PUTS - 892
2010-11-16-22_access.log - PUTS - 910
```

3. List the object names that begin with a specified string.

4. Run the **swift list -p 2010-11-15** command to list objects in the logtest container that begin with the 2010-11-15 string.

5. For each item in the list, run the **swift download -o -** command.

6. Pipe the output to **grep** and **wc**. Use the **echo** command to display the object name.

```
$ for f in `swift -A http://swift-auth.com:11000/v1.0 -U test:tester \
 -K testing list -p 2010-11-15 logtest` ; \
        do  echo -ne "$f - PUTS - " ; swift -A \
        http://127.0.0.1:11000/v1.0 -U test:tester \
        -K testing download -o - logtest $f | grep PUT | wc -l ; \
    done
```

```
2010-11-15-21_access.log - PUTS - 402
2010-11-15-22_access.log - PUTS - 910
```

4.15 Manage Block Storage scheduling

As an administrative user, you have some control over which volume back end your volumes reside on. You can specify affinity or anti-affinity between two volumes. Affinity between volumes means that they are stored on the same back end, whereas anti-affinity means that they are stored on different back ends.

For information on how to set up multiple back ends for Cinder, refer to the guide for Configuring multiple-storage back ends (http://docs.openstack.org/admin-guide-cloud/blockstorage_multi_backend.html) ↗.

4.15.1 Example Usages

1. Create new volume on the same back end as Volume_A:

   ```
   $ cinder create --hint same_host=Volume_A-UUID SIZE
   ```

2. Create new volume on a different back end than Volume_A:

   ```
   $ cinder create --hint different_host=Volume_A-UUID SIZE
   ```

3. Create new volume on the same back end as Volume_A and Volume_B:

   ```
   $ cinder create --hint same_host=Volume_A-UUID --hint same_host=Volume_B-UUID
     SIZE
   ```

   Or:

   ```
   $ cinder create --hint same_host="[Volume_A-UUID, Volume_B-UUID]" SIZE
   ```

4. Create new volume on a different back end than both Volume_A and Volume_B:

   ```
   $ cinder create --hint different_host=Volume_A-UUID --hint different_host=Volume_B-UUID
     SIZE
   ```

   Or:

   ```
   $ cinder create --hint different_host="[Volume_A-UUID, Volume_B-UUID]" SIZE
   ```

5 Community support

The following resources are available to help you run and use OpenStack. The OpenStack community constantly improves and adds to the main features of OpenStack, but if you have any questions, do not hesitate to ask. Use the following resources to get OpenStack support, and troubleshoot your installations.

5.1 Documentation

For the available OpenStack documentation, see docs.openstack.org (http://docs.openstack.org) ↗.

To provide feedback on documentation, join and use the openstack-docs@lists.openstack.org (mailto:openstack-docs@lists.openstack.org) ↗ mailing list at OpenStack Documentation Mailing List (http://lists.openstack.org/cgi-bin/mailman/listinfo/openstack-docs) ↗, or report a bug (https://bugs.launchpad.net/openstack-manuals/+filebug) ↗.

The following books explain how to install an OpenStack cloud and its associated components:

- Installation Guide for openSUSE 13.2 and SUSE Linux Enterprise Server 12 (http://docs.openstack.org/liberty/install-guide-obs/) ↗

- Installation Guide for Red Hat Enterprise Linux 7 and CentOS 7 (http://docs.openstack.org/liberty/install-guide-rdo/) ↗

- Installation Guide for Ubuntu 14.04 (http://docs.openstack.org/liberty/install-guide-ubuntu/) ↗

The following books explain how to configure and run an OpenStack cloud:

- Architecture Design Guide (http://docs.openstack.org/arch-design/) ↗

- Cloud Administrator Guide (http://docs.openstack.org/admin-guide-cloud/) ↗

- Configuration Reference (http://docs.openstack.org/liberty/config-reference/content/) ↗

- Operations Guide (http://docs.openstack.org/ops/) ↗

- Networking Guide (http://docs.openstack.org/liberty/networking-guide) ↗

- High Availability Guide (http://docs.openstack.org/ha-guide/) ↗

- Security Guide (http://docs.openstack.org/sec/) ↗

- Virtual Machine Image Guide (http://docs.openstack.org/image-guide/) ↗

The following books explain how to use the OpenStack dashboard and command-line clients:

- API Guide (http://developer.openstack.org/api-guide/quick-start/) ↗

- End User Guide (http://docs.openstack.org/user-guide/) ↗

- Admin User Guide (http://docs.openstack.org/user-guide-admin/) ↗

- Command-Line Interface Reference (http://docs.openstack.org/cli-reference/) ↗

The following documentation provides reference and guidance information for the OpenStack APIs:

- OpenStack API Complete Reference (HTML) (http://developer.openstack.org/api-ref.html) ↗

- API Complete Reference (PDF) (http://developer.openstack.org/api-ref-guides/bk-api-ref.pdf) ↗

The following guide provides how to contribute to OpenStack documentation:

- Documentation contributor guide (http://docs.openstack.org/contributor-guide/) ↗

5.2 ask.openstack.org

During the set up or testing of OpenStack, you might have questions about how a specific task is completed or be in a situation where a feature does not work correctly. Use the ask.openstack.org (https://ask.openstack.org) ↗ site to ask questions and get answers. When you visit the https://ask.openstack.org ↗ site, scan the recently asked questions to see whether your question has already been answered. If not, ask a new question. Be sure to give a clear, concise summary in the title and provide as much detail as possible in the description. Paste in your command output or stack traces, links to screen shots, and any other information which might be useful.

5.3 OpenStack mailing lists

A great way to get answers and insights is to post your question or problematic scenario to the OpenStack mailing list. You can learn from and help others who might have similar issues. To subscribe or view the archives, go to http://lists.openstack.org/cgi-bin/mailman/listinfo/openstack ↗. You might be interested in the other mailing lists for specific projects or development, which you can find on the wiki (https://wiki.openstack.org/wiki/MailingLists) ↗. A description of all mailing lists is available at https://wiki.openstack.org/wiki/MailingLists ↗.

5.4   The OpenStack wiki

The OpenStack wiki (https://wiki.openstack.org/) ↗ contains a broad range of topics but some of the information can be difficult to find or is a few pages deep. Fortunately, the wiki search feature enables you to search by title or content. If you search for specific information, such as about networking or OpenStack Compute, you can find a large amount of relevant material. More is being added all the time, so be sure to check back often. You can find the search box in the upper-right corner of any OpenStack wiki page.

5.5   The Launchpad Bugs area

The OpenStack community values your set up and testing efforts and wants your feedback. To log a bug, you must sign up for a Launchpad account at https://launchpad.net/+login ↗. You can view existing bugs and report bugs in the Launchpad Bugs area. Use the search feature to determine whether the bug has already been reported or already been fixed. If it still seems like your bug is unreported, fill out a bug report.

Some tips:

- Give a clear, concise summary.

- Provide as much detail as possible in the description. Paste in your command output or stack traces, links to screen shots, and any other information which might be useful.

- Be sure to include the software and package versions that you are using, especially if you are using a development branch, such as, `"Kilo release" vs git commit bc79c3ecc55929bac585d04a03475b72e06a3208`.

- Any deployment-specific information is helpful, such as whether you are using Ubuntu 14.04 or are performing a multi-node installation.

The following Launchpad Bugs areas are available:

- Bugs: OpenStack Block Storage (cinder) (https://bugs.launchpad.net/cinder) ↗

- Bugs: OpenStack Compute (nova) (https://bugs.launchpad.net/nova) ↗

- Bugs: OpenStack Dashboard (horizon) (https://bugs.launchpad.net/horizon) ↗

- Bugs: OpenStack Identity (keystone) (https://bugs.launchpad.net/keystone) ↗

- Bugs: OpenStack Image service (glance) (https://bugs.launchpad.net/glance) ↗

- Bugs: OpenStack Networking (neutron) (https://bugs.launchpad.net/neutron) ↗

- Bugs: OpenStack Object Storage (swift) (https://bugs.launchpad.net/swift) ↗

- Bugs: Application catalog (murano) (https://bugs.launchpad.net/murano) ↗

- Bugs: Bare metal service (ironic) (https://bugs.launchpad.net/ironic) ↗

- Bugs: Clustering service (senlin) (https://bugs.launchpad.net/senlin) ↗

- Bugs: Containers service (magnum) (https://bugs.launchpad.net/magnum) ↗

- Bugs: Data processing service (sahara) (https://bugs.launchpad.net/sahara) ↗

- Bugs: Database service (trove) (https://bugs.launchpad.net/trove) ↗

- Bugs: Deployment service (fuel) (https://bugs.launchpad.net/fuel) ↗

- Bugs: DNS service (designate) (https://bugs.launchpad.net/designate) ↗

- Bugs: Key Manager Service (barbican) (https://bugs.launchpad.net/barbican) ↗

- Bugs: Monitoring (monasca) (https://bugs.launchpad.net/monasca) ↗

- Bugs: Orchestration (heat) (https://bugs.launchpad.net/heat) ↗

- Bugs: Rating (cloudkitty) (https://bugs.launchpad.net/cloudkitty) ↗

- Bugs: Shared file systems (manila) (https://bugs.launchpad.net/manila) ↗

- Bugs: Telemetry (ceilometer) (https://bugs.launchpad.net/ceilometer) ↗

- Bugs: Telemetry v3 (gnocchi) (https://bugs.launchpad.net/gnocchi) ↗

- Bugs: Workflow service (mistral) (https://bugs.launchpad.net/mistral) ↗

- Bugs: Messaging service (zaqar) (https://bugs.launchpad.net/zaqar) ↗

- Bugs: OpenStack API Documentation (developer.openstack.org) (https://bugs.launchpad.net/openstack-api-site) ↗

- Bugs: OpenStack Documentation (docs.openstack.org) (https://bugs.launchpad.net/openstack-manuals) ↗

5.6   The OpenStack IRC channel

The OpenStack community lives in the #openstack IRC channel on the Freenode network. You can hang out, ask questions, or get immediate feedback for urgent and pressing issues. To install an IRC client or use a browser-based client, go to https://webchat.freenode.net/ (https://webchat.freenode.net) ↗. You can also use Colloquy (Mac OS X, http://colloquy.info/ ↗), mIRC (Windows, http://www.mirc.com/ ↗), or XChat (Linux). When you are in the IRC channel and want to share code or command output, the generally accepted method is to use a Paste Bin. The OpenStack project has one at http://paste.openstack.org ↗. Just paste your longer amounts of text or logs in the web form and you get a URL that you can paste into the channel. The OpenStack IRC channel is `#openstack` on `irc.freenode.net`. You can find a list of all OpenStack IRC channels at https://wiki.openstack.org/wiki/IRC ↗.

5.7   Documentation feedback

To provide feedback on documentation, join and use the openstack-docs@lists.openstack.org (mailto:openstack-docs@lists.openstack.org) ↗ mailing list at OpenStack Documentation Mailing List (http://lists.openstack.org/cgi-bin/mailman/listinfo/openstack-docs) ↗, or report a bug (https://bugs.launchpad.net/openstack-manuals/+filebug) ↗.

5.8   OpenStack distribution packages

The following Linux distributions provide community-supported packages for OpenStack:

- **Debian:** https://wiki.debian.org/OpenStack ↗

- **CentOS, Fedora, and Red Hat Enterprise Linux:** https://www.rdoproject.org/ ↗

- **openSUSE and SUSE Linux Enterprise Server:** https://en.opensuse.org/ Portal:OpenStack ↗

- **Ubuntu:** https://wiki.ubuntu.com/ServerTeam/CloudArchive ↗

Glossary

This glossary offers a list of terms and definitions to define a vocabulary for OpenStack-related concepts.

To add to OpenStack glossary, clone the openstack/openstack-manuals repository (https://git.openstack.org/cgit/openstack/openstack-manuals) ↗ and update the source file `doc/glossary/glossary-terms.xml` through the OpenStack contribution process.

6to4

A mechanism that allows IPv6 packets to be transmitted over an IPv4 network, providing a strategy for migrating to IPv6.

absolute limit

Impassable limits for guest VMs. Settings include total RAM size, maximum number of vCPUs, and maximum disk size.

access control list

A list of permissions attached to an object. An ACL specifies which users or system processes have access to objects. It also defines which operations can be performed on specified objects. Each entry in a typical ACL specifies a subject and an operation. For instance, the ACL entry `(Alice, delete)` for a file gives Alice permission to delete the file.

access key

Alternative term for an Amazon EC2 access key. See EC2 access key.

account

The Object Storage context of an account. Do not confuse with a user account from an authentication service, such as Active Directory, /etc/passwd, OpenLDAP, OpenStack Identity, and so on.

account auditor

Checks for missing replicas and incorrect or corrupted objects in a specified Object Storage account by running queries against the back-end SQLite database.

account database

A SQLite database that contains Object Storage accounts and related metadata and that the accounts server accesses.

account reaper

An Object Storage worker that scans for and deletes account databases and that the account server has marked for deletion.

account server

Lists containers in Object Storage and stores container information in the account database.

account service

An Object Storage component that provides account services such as list, create, modify, and audit. Do not confuse with OpenStack Identity service, OpenLDAP, or similar user-account services.

accounting

The Compute service provides accounting information through the event notification and system usage data facilities.

ACL

See access control list.

active/active configuration

In a high-availability setup with an active/active configuration, several systems share the load together and if one fails, the load is distributed to the remaining systems.

Active Directory

Authentication and identity service by Microsoft, based on LDAP. Supported in OpenStack.

active/passive configuration

In a high-availability setup with an active/passive configuration, systems are set up to bring additional resources online to replace those that have failed.

address pool

A group of fixed and/or floating IP addresses that are assigned to a project and can be used by or assigned to the VM instances in a project.

admin API

A subset of API calls that are accessible to authorized administrators and are generally not accessible to end users or the public Internet. They can exist as a separate service (keystone) or can be a subset of another API (nova).

admin server

In the context of the Identity service, the worker process that provides access to the admin API.

Advanced Message Queuing Protocol (AMQP)

The open standard messaging protocol used by OpenStack components for intra-service communications, provided by RabbitMQ, Qpid, or ZeroMQ.

Advanced RISC Machine (ARM)

Lower power consumption CPU often found in mobile and embedded devices. Supported by OpenStack.

alert

The Compute service can send alerts through its notification system, which includes a facility to create custom notification drivers. Alerts can be sent to and displayed on the horizon dashboard.

allocate

The process of taking a floating IP address from the address pool so it can be associated with a fixed IP on a guest VM instance.

Amazon Kernel Image (AKI)

Both a VM container format and disk format. Supported by Image service.

Amazon Machine Image (AMI)

Both a VM container format and disk format. Supported by Image service.

Amazon Ramdisk Image (ARI)

Both a VM container format and disk format. Supported by Image service.

Anvil

A project that ports the shell script-based project named DevStack to Python.

Apache

The Apache Software Foundation supports the Apache community of open-source software projects. These projects provide software products for the public good.

Apache License 2.0

All OpenStack core projects are provided under the terms of the Apache License 2.0 license.

Apache Web Server

The most common web server software currently used on the Internet.

API endpoint

The daemon, worker, or service that a client communicates with to access an API. API endpoints can provide any number of services, such as authentication, sales data, performance meters, Compute VM commands, census data, and so on.

API extension

Custom modules that extend some OpenStack core APIs.

API extension plug-in

Alternative term for a Networking plug-in or Networking API extension.

API key

Alternative term for an API token.

API server

Any node running a daemon or worker that provides an API endpoint.

API token

Passed to API requests and used by OpenStack to verify that the client is authorized to run the requested operation.

API version

In OpenStack, the API version for a project is part of the URL. For example, `example.com/nova/v1/foobar`.

applet

A Java program that can be embedded into a web page.

Application Programming Interface (API)

A collection of specifications used to access a service, application, or program. Includes service calls, required parameters for each call, and the expected return values.

Application catalog

OpenStack project that provides an application catalog service so that users can compose and deploy composite environments on an application abstraction level while managing the application lifecycle. The code name of the project is murano.

application server

A piece of software that makes available another piece of software over a network.

Application Service Provider (ASP)

Companies that rent specialized applications that help businesses and organizations provide additional services with lower cost.

Address Resolution Protocol (ARP)

The protocol by which layer-3 IP addresses are resolved into layer-2 link local addresses.

arptables

Tool used for maintaining Address Resolution Protocol packet filter rules in the Linux kernel firewall modules. Used along with iptables, ebtables, and ip6tables in Compute to provide firewall services for VMs.

associate

The process associating a Compute floating IP address with a fixed IP address.

Asynchronous JavaScript and XML (AJAX)

A group of interrelated web development techniques used on the client-side to create asynchronous web applications. Used extensively in horizon.

ATA over Ethernet (AoE)

A disk storage protocol tunneled within Ethernet.

attach

The process of connecting a VIF or vNIC to a L2 network in Networking. In the context of Compute, this process connects a storage volume to an instance.

attachment (network)

Association of an interface ID to a logical port. Plugs an interface into a port.

auditing

Provided in Compute through the system usage data facility.

auditor

A worker process that verifies the integrity of Object Storage objects, containers, and accounts. Auditors is the collective term for the Object Storage account auditor, container auditor, and object auditor.

Austin

The code name for the initial release of OpenStack. The first design summit took place in Austin, Texas, US.

auth node

Alternative term for an Object Storage authorization node.

authentication

The process that confirms that the user, process, or client is really who they say they are through private key, secret token, password, fingerprint, or similar method.

authentication token

A string of text provided to the client after authentication. Must be provided by the user or process in subsequent requests to the API endpoint.

AuthN

The Identity service component that provides authentication services.

authorization

The act of verifying that a user, process, or client is authorized to perform an action.

authorization node

An Object Storage node that provides authorization services.

AuthZ

The Identity component that provides high-level authorization services.

Auto ACK

Configuration setting within RabbitMQ that enables or disables message acknowledgment. Enabled by default.

auto declare

A Compute RabbitMQ setting that determines whether a message exchange is automatically created when the program starts.

availability zone

An Amazon EC2 concept of an isolated area that is used for fault tolerance. Do not confuse with an OpenStack Compute zone or cell.

AWS

Amazon Web Services.

AWS CloudFormation template

AWS CloudFormation allows AWS users to create and manage a collection of related resources. The Orchestration service supports a CloudFormation-compatible format (CFN).

back end

Interactions and processes that are obfuscated from the user, such as Compute volume mount, data transmission to an iSCSI target by a daemon, or Object Storage object integrity checks.

back-end catalog

The storage method used by the Identity service catalog service to store and retrieve information about API endpoints that are available to the client. Examples include a SQL database, LDAP database, or KVS back end.

back-end store

The persistent data store used to save and retrieve information for a service, such as lists of Object Storage objects, current state of guest VMs, lists of user names, and so on. Also, the method that the Image service uses to get and store VM images. Options include Object Storage, local file system, S3, and HTTP.

backup restore and disaster recovery as a service

The OpenStack project that provides integrated tooling for backing up, restoring, and recovering file systems, instances, or database backups. The project name is freezer.

bandwidth

The amount of available data used by communication resources, such as the Internet. Represents the amount of data that is used to download things or the amount of data available to download.

barbican

Code name of the key management service for OpenStack.

bare

An Image service container format that indicates that no container exists for the VM image.

Bare metal service

OpenStack project that provisions bare metal, as opposed to virtual, machines. The code name for the project is ironic.

base image

An OpenStack-provided image.

Bell-LaPadula model

A security model that focuses on data confidentiality and controlled access to classified information. This model divide the entities into subjects and objects. The clearance of a subject is compared to the classification of the object to determine if the subject is authorized for the specific access mode. The clearance or classification scheme is expressed in terms of a lattice.

Benchmark service

OpenStack project that provides a framework for performance analysis and benchmarking of individual OpenStack components as well as full production OpenStack cloud deployments. The code name of the project is rally.

Bexar

A grouped release of projects related to OpenStack that came out in February of 2011. It included only Compute (nova) and Object Storage (swift). Bexar is the code name for the second release of OpenStack. The design summit took place in San Antonio, Texas, US, which is the county seat for Bexar county.

binary

Information that consists solely of ones and zeroes, which is the language of computers.

bit

A bit is a single digit number that is in base of 2 (either a zero or one). Bandwidth usage is measured in bits per second.

bits per second (BPS)

The universal measurement of how quickly data is transferred from place to place.

block device

A device that moves data in the form of blocks. These device nodes interface the devices, such as hard disks, CD-ROM drives, flash drives, and other addressable regions of memory.

block migration

A method of VM live migration used by KVM to evacuate instances from one host to another with very little downtime during a user-initiated switchover. Does not require shared storage. Supported by Compute.

Block Storage

The OpenStack core project that enables management of volumes, volume snapshots, and volume types. The project name of Block Storage is cinder.

Block Storage API

An API on a separate endpoint for attaching, detaching, and creating block storage for compute VMs.

BMC

Baseboard Management Controller. The intelligence in the IPMI architecture, which is a specialized micro-controller that is embedded on the motherboard of a computer and acts as a server. Manages the interface between system management software and platform hardware.

bootable disk image

A type of VM image that exists as a single, bootable file.

Bootstrap Protocol (BOOTP)

A network protocol used by a network client to obtain an IP address from a configuration server. Provided in Compute through the dnsmasq daemon when using either the FlatDHCP manager or VLAN manager network manager.

Border Gateway Protocol (BGP)

The Border Gateway Protocol is a dynamic routing protocol that connects autonomous systems. Considered the backbone of the Internet, this protocol connects disparate networks to form a larger network.

browser

Any client software that enables a computer or device to access the Internet.

builder file

Contains configuration information that Object Storage uses to reconfigure a ring or to recreate it from scratch after a serious failure.

bursting

The practice of utilizing a secondary environment to elastically build instances on-demand when the primary environment is resource constrained.

button class

A group of related button types within horizon. Buttons to start, stop, and suspend VMs are in one class. Buttons to associate and disassociate floating IP addresses are in another class, and so on.

byte

Set of bits that make up a single character; there are usually 8 bits to a byte.

CA

Certificate Authority or Certification Authority. In cryptography, an entity that issues digital certificates. The digital certificate certifies the ownership of a public key by the named subject of the certificate. This enables others (relying parties) to rely upon signatures or assertions made by the private key that corresponds to the certified public key. In this model of trust relationships, a CA is a trusted third party for both the subject (owner) of the certificate and the party relying upon the certificate. CAs are characteristic of many public key infrastructure (PKI) schemes.

cache pruner

A program that keeps the Image service VM image cache at or below its configured maximum size.

Cactus

An OpenStack grouped release of projects that came out in the spring of 2011. It included Compute (nova), Object Storage (swift), and the Image service (glance). Cactus is a city in Texas, US and is the code name for the third release of OpenStack. When OpenStack releases went from three to six months long, the code name of the release changed to match a geography nearest the previous summit.

CADF

Cloud Auditing Data Federation (CADF) is a specification for audit event data. CADF is supported by OpenStack Identity.

CALL

One of the RPC primitives used by the OpenStack message queue software. Sends a message and waits for a response.

capability

Defines resources for a cell, including CPU, storage, and networking. Can apply to the specific services within a cell or a whole cell.

capacity cache

A Compute back-end database table that contains the current workload, amount of free RAM, and number of VMs running on each host. Used to determine on which host a VM starts.

capacity updater

A notification driver that monitors VM instances and updates the capacity cache as needed.

CAST

One of the RPC primitives used by the OpenStack message queue software. Sends a message and does not wait for a response.

catalog

A list of API endpoints that are available to a user after authentication with the Identity service.

catalog service

An Identity service that lists API endpoints that are available to a user after authentication with the Identity service.

ceilometer

The project name for the Telemetry service, which is an integrated project that provides metering and measuring facilities for OpenStack.

cell

Provides logical partitioning of Compute resources in a child and parent relationship. Requests are passed from parent cells to child cells if the parent cannot provide the requested resource.

cell forwarding

A Compute option that enables parent cells to pass resource requests to child cells if the parent cannot provide the requested resource.

cell manager

The Compute component that contains a list of the current capabilities of each host within the cell and routes requests as appropriate.

CentOS

A Linux distribution that is compatible with OpenStack.

Ceph

Massively scalable distributed storage system that consists of an object store, block store, and POSIX-compatible distributed file system. Compatible with OpenStack.

CephFS

The POSIX-compliant file system provided by Ceph.

certificate authority

A simple certificate authority provided by Compute for cloudpipe VPNs and VM image decryption.

Challenge-Handshake Authentication Protocol (CHAP)

An iSCSI authentication method supported by Compute.

chance scheduler

A scheduling method used by Compute that randomly chooses an available host from the pool.

changes since

A Compute API parameter that downloads changes to the requested item since your last request, instead of downloading a new, fresh set of data and comparing it against the old data.

Chef

An operating system configuration management tool supporting OpenStack deployments.

child cell

If a requested resource such as CPU time, disk storage, or memory is not available in the parent cell, the request is forwarded to its associated child cells. If the child cell can fulfill the request, it does. Otherwise, it attempts to pass the request to any of its children.

cinder

A core OpenStack project that provides block storage services for VMs.

CirrOS

A minimal Linux distribution designed for use as a test image on clouds such as OpenStack.

Cisco neutron plug-in

A Networking plug-in for Cisco devices and technologies, including UCS and Nexus.

cloud architect

A person who plans, designs, and oversees the creation of clouds.

cloud computing

A model that enables access to a shared pool of configurable computing resources, such as networks, servers, storage, applications, and services, that can be rapidly provisioned and released with minimal management effort or service provider interaction.

cloud controller

Collection of Compute components that represent the global state of the cloud; talks to services, such as Identity authentication, Object Storage, and node/storage workers through a queue.

cloud controller node

A node that runs network, volume, API, scheduler, and image services. Each service may be broken out into separate nodes for scalability or availability.

Cloud Data Management Interface (CDMI)

SINA standard that defines a RESTful API for managing objects in the cloud, currently unsupported in OpenStack.

Cloud Infrastructure Management Interface (CIMI)

An in-progress specification for cloud management. Currently unsupported in OpenStack.

cloud-init

A package commonly installed in VM images that performs initialization of an instance after boot using information that it retrieves from the metadata service, such as the SSH public key and user data.

cloudadmin

One of the default roles in the Compute RBAC system. Grants complete system access.

Cloudbase-Init

A Windows project providing guest initialization features, similar to cloud-init.

cloudpipe

A compute service that creates VPNs on a per-project basis.

cloudpipe image

A pre-made VM image that serves as a cloudpipe server. Essentially, OpenVPN running on Linux.

Clustering

The OpenStack project that OpenStack project that implements clustering services and libraries for the management of groups of homogeneous objects exposed by other OpenStack services. The project name of Clustering service is senlin.

CMDB

Configuration Management Database.

congress

OpenStack project that provides the Governance service.

command filter

Lists allowed commands within the Compute rootwrap facility.

Common Internet File System (CIFS)

A file sharing protocol. It is a public or open variation of the original Server Message Block (SMB) protocol developed and used by Microsoft. Like the SMB protocol, CIFS runs at a higher level and uses the TCP/IP protocol.

community project

A project that is not officially endorsed by the OpenStack Foundation. If the project is successful enough, it might be elevated to an incubated project and then to a core project, or it might be merged with the main code trunk.

compression

Reducing the size of files by special encoding, the file can be decompressed again to its original content. OpenStack supports compression at the Linux file system level but does not support compression for things such as Object Storage objects or Image service VM images.

Compute

The OpenStack core project that provides compute services. The project name of Compute service is nova.

Compute API

The nova-api daemon provides access to nova services. Can communicate with other APIs, such as the Amazon EC2 API.

compute controller

The Compute component that chooses suitable hosts on which to start VM instances.

compute host

Physical host dedicated to running compute nodes.

compute node

A node that runs the nova-compute daemon that manages VM instances that provide a wide range of services, such as web applications and analytics.

Compute service

Name for the Compute component that manages VMs.

compute worker

The Compute component that runs on each compute node and manages the VM instance life cycle, including run, reboot, terminate, attach/detach volumes, and so on. Provided by the nova-compute daemon.

concatenated object

A set of segment objects that Object Storage combines and sends to the client.

conductor

In Compute, conductor is the process that proxies database requests from the compute process. Using conductor improves security because compute nodes do not need direct access to the database.

consistency window

The amount of time it takes for a new Object Storage object to become accessible to all clients.

console log

Contains the output from a Linux VM console in Compute.

container

Organizes and stores objects in Object Storage. Similar to the concept of a Linux directory but cannot be nested. Alternative term for an Image service container format.

container auditor

Checks for missing replicas or incorrect objects in specified Object Storage containers through queries to the SQLite back-end database.

container database

A SQLite database that stores Object Storage containers and container metadata. The container server accesses this database.

container format

A wrapper used by the Image service that contains a VM image and its associated metadata, such as machine state, OS disk size, and so on.

container server

An Object Storage server that manages containers.

Containers service

OpenStack project that provides a set of services for management of application containers in a multi-tenant cloud environment. The code name of the project name is magnum.

container service

The Object Storage component that provides container services, such as create, delete, list, and so on.

content delivery network (CDN)

A content delivery network is a specialized network that is used to distribute content to clients, typically located close to the client for increased performance.

controller node

Alternative term for a cloud controller node.

core API

Depending on context, the core API is either the OpenStack API or the main API of a specific core project, such as Compute, Networking, Image service, and so on.

core project

An official OpenStack project. Currently consists of Compute (nova), Object Storage (swift), Image service (glance), Identity (keystone), Dashboard (horizon), Networking (neutron), and Block Storage (cinder), Telemetry (ceilometer), Orchestration (heat), Database service (trove), Bare Metal service (ironic), Data processing service (sahara). However, this definition is changing based on community discussions about the "Big Tent".

cost

Under the Compute distributed scheduler, this is calculated by looking at the capabilities of each host relative to the flavor of the VM instance being requested.

credentials

Data that is only known to or accessible by a user and used to verify that the user is who he says he is. Credentials are presented to the server during authentication. Examples include a password, secret key, digital certificate, and fingerprint.

Cross-Origin Resource Sharing (CORS)

A mechanism that allows many resources (for example, fonts, JavaScript) on a web page to be requested from another domain outside the domain from which the resource originated. In particular, JavaScript's AJAX calls can use the XMLHttpRequest mechanism.

Crowbar

An open source community project by Dell that aims to provide all necessary services to quickly deploy clouds.

current workload

An element of the Compute capacity cache that is calculated based on the number of build, snapshot, migrate, and resize operations currently in progress on a given host.

customer

Alternative term for tenant.

customization module

A user-created Python module that is loaded by horizon to change the look and feel of the dashboard.

daemon

A process that runs in the background and waits for requests. May or may not listen on a TCP or UDP port. Do not confuse with a worker.

DAC

Discretionary access control. Governs the ability of subjects to access objects, while enabling users to make policy decisions and assign security attributes. The traditional UNIX system of users, groups, and read-write-execute permissions is an example of DAC.

dashboard

The web-based management interface for OpenStack. An alternative name for horizon.

data encryption

Both Image service and Compute support encrypted virtual machine (VM) images (but not instances). In-transit data encryption is supported in OpenStack using technologies such as HTTPS, SSL, TLS, and SSH. Object Storage does not support object encryption at the application level but may support storage that uses disk encryption.

database ID

A unique ID given to each replica of an Object Storage database.

database replicator

An Object Storage component that copies changes in the account, container, and object databases to other nodes.

Database service

An integrated project that provide scalable and reliable Cloud Database-as-a-Service functionality for both relational and non-relational database engines. The project name of Database service is trove.

Data processing service

OpenStack project that provides a scalable data-processing stack and associated management interfaces. The code name for the project is sahara.

data store

A database engine supported by the Database service.

deallocate

The process of removing the association between a floating IP address and a fixed IP address. Once this association is removed, the floating IP returns to the address pool.

Debian

A Linux distribution that is compatible with OpenStack.

deduplication

The process of finding duplicate data at the disk block, file, and/or object level to minimize storage use—currently unsupported within OpenStack.

default panel

The default panel that is displayed when a user accesses the horizon dashboard.

default tenant

New users are assigned to this tenant if no tenant is specified when a user is created.

default token

An Identity service token that is not associated with a specific tenant and is exchanged for a scoped token.

delayed delete

An option within Image service so that an image is deleted after a predefined number of seconds instead of immediately.

delivery mode

Setting for the Compute RabbitMQ message delivery mode; can be set to either transient or persistent.

denial of service (DoS)

Denial of service (DoS) is a short form for denial-of-service attack. This is a malicious attempt to prevent legitimate users from using a service.

deprecated auth

An option within Compute that enables administrators to create and manage users through the `nova-manage` command as opposed to using the Identity service.

Designate

Code name for the DNS service project for OpenStack.

Desktop-as-a-Service

A platform that provides a suite of desktop environments that users access to receive a desktop experience from any location. This may provide general use, development, or even homogeneous testing environments.

developer

One of the default roles in the Compute RBAC system and the default role assigned to a new user.

device ID

Maps Object Storage partitions to physical storage devices.

device weight

Distributes partitions proportionately across Object Storage devices based on the storage capacity of each device.

DevStack

Community project that uses shell scripts to quickly build complete OpenStack development environments.

DHCP

Dynamic Host Configuration Protocol. A network protocol that configures devices that are connected to a network so that they can communicate on that network by using the Internet Protocol (IP). The protocol is implemented in a client-server model where DHCP clients request configuration data, such as an IP address, a default route, and one or more DNS server addresses from a DHCP server.

DHCP agent

OpenStack Networking agent that provides DHCP services for virtual networks.

Diablo

A grouped release of projects related to OpenStack that came out in the fall of 2011, the fourth release of OpenStack. It included Compute (nova 2011.3), Object Storage (swift 1.4.3), and the Image service (glance). Diablo is the code name for the fourth release of OpenStack. The design summit took place in in the Bay Area near Santa Clara, California, US and Diablo is a nearby city.

direct consumer

An element of the Compute RabbitMQ that comes to life when a RPC call is executed. It connects to a direct exchange through a unique exclusive queue, sends the message, and terminates.

direct exchange

A routing table that is created within the Compute RabbitMQ during RPC calls; one is created for each RPC call that is invoked.

direct publisher

Element of RabbitMQ that provides a response to an incoming MQ message.

disassociate

The process of removing the association between a floating IP address and fixed IP and thus returning the floating IP address to the address pool.

disk encryption

The ability to encrypt data at the file system, disk partition, or whole-disk level. Supported within Compute VMs.

disk format

The underlying format that a disk image for a VM is stored as within the Image service back-end store. For example, AMI, ISO, QCOW2, VMDK, and so on.

dispersion

In Object Storage, tools to test and ensure dispersion of objects and containers to ensure fault tolerance.

distributed virtual router (DVR)

Mechanism for highly-available multi-host routing when using OpenStack Networking (neutron).

Django

A web framework used extensively in horizon.

DNS

Domain Name System. A hierarchical and distributed naming system for computers, services, and resources connected to the Internet or a private network. Associates a human-friendly names to IP addresses.

DNS record

A record that specifies information about a particular domain and belongs to the domain.

DNS service

OpenStack project that provides scalable, on demand, self service access to authoritative DNS services, in a technology-agnostic manner. The code name for the project is designate.

dnsmasq

Daemon that provides DNS, DHCP, BOOTP, and TFTP services for virtual networks.

domain

An Identity API v3 entity. Represents a collection of projects, groups and users that defines administrative boundaries for managing OpenStack Identity entities. On the Internet, separates a website from other sites. Often, the domain name has two or more parts that are separated by dots. For example, yahoo.com, usa.gov, harvard.edu, or mail.yahoo.com. Also, a domain is an entity or container of all DNS-related information containing one or more records.

Domain Name System (DNS)

A system by which Internet domain name-to-address and address-to-name resolutions are determined. DNS helps navigate the Internet by translating the IP address into an address that is easier to remember. For example, translating 111.111.111.1 into www.yahoo.com. All domains and their components, such as mail servers, utilize DNS to resolve to the appropriate locations. DNS servers are usually set up in a master-slave relationship such that failure of the master invokes the slave. DNS servers might also be clustered or replicated such that changes made to one DNS server are automatically propagated to other active servers. In Compute, the support that enables associating DNS entries with floating IP addresses, nodes, or cells so that hostnames are consistent across reboots.

download

The transfer of data, usually in the form of files, from one computer to another.

DRTM

Dynamic root of trust measurement.

durable exchange

The Compute RabbitMQ message exchange that remains active when the server restarts.

durable queue

A Compute RabbitMQ message queue that remains active when the server restarts.

Dynamic Host Configuration Protocol (DHCP)

A method to automatically configure networking for a host at boot time. Provided by both Networking and Compute.

Dynamic HyperText Markup Language (DHTML)

Pages that use HTML, JavaScript, and Cascading Style Sheets to enable users to interact with a web page or show simple animation.

east-west traffic

Network traffic between servers in the same cloud or data center. See also north-south traffic.

EBS boot volume

An Amazon EBS storage volume that contains a bootable VM image, currently unsupported in OpenStack.

ebtables

Filtering tool for a Linux bridging firewall, enabling filtering of network traffic passing through a Linux bridge. Used in Compute along with arptables, iptables, and ip6tables to ensure isolation of network communications.

EC2

The Amazon commercial compute product, similar to Compute.

EC2 access key

Used along with an EC2 secret key to access the Compute EC2 API.

EC2 API

OpenStack supports accessing the Amazon EC2 API through Compute.

EC2 Compatibility API

A Compute component that enables OpenStack to communicate with Amazon EC2.

EC2 secret key

Used along with an EC2 access key when communicating with the Compute EC2 API; used to digitally sign each request.

Elastic Block Storage (EBS)

The Amazon commercial block storage product.

encryption

OpenStack supports encryption technologies such as HTTPS, SSH, SSL, TLS, digital certificates, and data encryption.

endpoint

See API endpoint.

endpoint registry

Alternative term for an Identity service catalog.

encapsulation

The practice of placing one packet type within another for the purposes of abstracting or securing data. Examples include GRE, MPLS, or IPsec.

endpoint template

A list of URL and port number endpoints that indicate where a service, such as Object Storage, Compute, Identity, and so on, can be accessed.

entity

Any piece of hardware or software that wants to connect to the network services provided by Networking, the network connectivity service. An entity can make use of Networking by implementing a VIF.

ephemeral image

A VM image that does not save changes made to its volumes and reverts them to their original state after the instance is terminated.

ephemeral volume

Volume that does not save the changes made to it and reverts to its original state when the current user relinquishes control.

Essex

A grouped release of projects related to OpenStack that came out in April 2012, the fifth release of OpenStack. It included Compute (nova 2012.1), Object Storage (swift 1.4.8), Image (glance), Identity (keystone), and Dashboard (horizon). Essex is the code name for the fifth release of OpenStack. The design summit took place in Boston, Massachusetts, US and Essex is a nearby city.

ESXi

An OpenStack-supported hypervisor.

ETag

MD5 hash of an object within Object Storage, used to ensure data integrity.

euca2ools

A collection of command-line tools for administering VMs; most are compatible with OpenStack.

Eucalyptus Kernel Image (EKI)

Used along with an ERI to create an EMI.

Eucalyptus Machine Image (EMI)

VM image container format supported by Image service.

Eucalyptus Ramdisk Image (ERI)

Used along with an EKI to create an EMI.

evacuate

The process of migrating one or all virtual machine (VM) instances from one host to another, compatible with both shared storage live migration and block migration.

exchange

Alternative term for a RabbitMQ message exchange.

exchange type

A routing algorithm in the Compute RabbitMQ.

exclusive queue

Connected to by a direct consumer in RabbitMQ—Compute, the message can be consumed only by the current connection.

extended attributes (xattr)

File system option that enables storage of additional information beyond owner, group, permissions, modification time, and so on. The underlying Object Storage file system must support extended attributes.

extension

Alternative term for an API extension or plug-in. In the context of Identity service, this is a call that is specific to the implementation, such as adding support for OpenID.

external network

A network segment typically used for instance Internet access.

extra specs

Specifies additional requirements when Compute determines where to start a new instance. Examples include a minimum amount of network bandwidth or a GPU.

FakeLDAP

An easy method to create a local LDAP directory for testing Identity and Compute. Requires Redis.

fan-out exchange

Within RabbitMQ and Compute, it is the messaging interface that is used by the scheduler service to receive capability messages from the compute, volume, and network nodes.

federated identity

A method to establish trusts between identity providers and the OpenStack cloud.

Fedora

A Linux distribution compatible with OpenStack.

Fibre Channel

Storage protocol similar in concept to TCP/IP; encapsulates SCSI commands and data.

Fibre Channel over Ethernet (FCoE)

The fibre channel protocol tunneled within Ethernet.

fill-first scheduler

The Compute scheduling method that attempts to fill a host with VMs rather than starting new VMs on a variety of hosts.

filter

The step in the Compute scheduling process when hosts that cannot run VMs are eliminated and not chosen.

firewall

Used to restrict communications between hosts and/or nodes, implemented in Compute using iptables, arptables, ip6tables, and ebtables.

FWaaS

A Networking extension that provides perimeter firewall functionality.

fixed IP address

An IP address that is associated with the same instance each time that instance boots, is generally not accessible to end users or the public Internet, and is used for management of the instance.

Flat Manager

The Compute component that gives IP addresses to authorized nodes and assumes DHCP, DNS, and routing configuration and services are provided by something else.

flat mode injection

A Compute networking method where the OS network configuration information is injected into the VM image before the instance starts.

flat network

Virtual network type that uses neither VLANs nor tunnels to segregate tenant traffic. Each flat network typically requires a separate underlying physical interface defined by bridge mappings. However, a flat network can contain multiple subnets.

FlatDHCP Manager

The Compute component that provides dnsmasq (DHCP, DNS, BOOTP, TFTP) and radvd (routing) services.

flavor

Alternative term for a VM instance type.

flavor ID

UUID for each Compute or Image service VM flavor or instance type.

floating IP address

An IP address that a project can associate with a VM so that the instance has the same public IP address each time that it boots. You create a pool of floating IP addresses and assign them to instances as they are launched to maintain a consistent IP address for maintaining DNS assignment.

Folsom

A grouped release of projects related to OpenStack that came out in the fall of 2012, the sixth release of OpenStack. It includes Compute (nova), Object Storage (swift), Identity (keystone), Networking (neutron), Image service (glance), and Volumes or Block Storage (cinder). Folsom is the code name for the sixth release of OpenStack. The design summit took place in San Francisco, California, US and Folsom is a nearby city.

FormPost

Object Storage middleware that uploads (posts) an image through a form on a web page.

freezer

OpenStack project that provides backup restore and disaster recovery as a service.

front end

The point where a user interacts with a service; can be an API endpoint, the horizon dashboard, or a command-line tool.

gateway

An IP address, typically assigned to a router, that passes network traffic between different networks.

generic receive offload (GRO)

Feature of certain network interface drivers that combines many smaller received packets into a large packet before delivery to the kernel IP stack.

generic routing encapsulation (GRE)

Protocol that encapsulates a wide variety of network layer protocols inside virtual point-to-point links.

glance

A core project that provides the OpenStack Image service.

glance API server

Processes client requests for VMs, updates Image service metadata on the registry server, and communicates with the store adapter to upload VM images from the back-end store.

glance registry

Alternative term for the Image service image registry.

global endpoint template

The Identity service endpoint template that contains services available to all tenants.

GlusterFS

A file system designed to aggregate NAS hosts, compatible with OpenStack.

golden image

A method of operating system installation where a finalized disk image is created and then used by all nodes without modification.

Governance service

OpenStack project to provide Governance-as-a-Service across any collection of cloud services in order to monitor, enforce, and audit policy over dynamic infrastructure. The code name for the project is congress.

Graphic Interchange Format (GIF)

A type of image file that is commonly used for animated images on web pages.

Graphics Processing Unit (GPU)

Choosing a host based on the existence of a GPU is currently unsupported in OpenStack.

Green Threads

The cooperative threading model used by Python; reduces race conditions and only context switches when specific library calls are made. Each OpenStack service is its own thread.

Grizzly

The code name for the seventh release of OpenStack. The design summit took place in San Diego, California, US and Grizzly is an element of the state flag of California.

Group

An Identity v3 API entity. Represents a collection of users that is owned by a specific domain.

guest OS

An operating system instance running under the control of a hypervisor.

Hadoop

Apache Hadoop is an open source software framework that supports data-intensive distributed applications.

Hadoop Distributed File System (HDFS)

A distributed, highly fault-tolerant file system designed to run on low-cost commodity hardware.

handover

An object state in Object Storage where a new replica of the object is automatically created due to a drive failure.

hard reboot

A type of reboot where a physical or virtual power button is pressed as opposed to a graceful, proper shutdown of the operating system.

Havana

The code name for the eighth release of OpenStack. The design summit took place in Portland, Oregon, US and Havana is an unincorporated community in Oregon.

heat

An integrated project that aims to orchestrate multiple cloud applications for OpenStack.

Heat Orchestration Template (HOT)

Heat input in the format native to OpenStack.

health monitor

Determines whether back-end members of a VIP pool can process a request. A pool can have several health monitors associated with it. When a pool has several monitors associated with it, all monitors check each member of the pool. All monitors must declare a member to be healthy for it to stay active.

high availability (HA)

A high availability system design approach and associated service implementation ensures that a prearranged level of operational performance will be met during a contractual measurement period. High availability systems seeks to minimize system downtime and data loss.

horizon

OpenStack project that provides a dashboard, which is a web interface.

horizon plug-in

A plug-in for the OpenStack dashboard (horizon).

host

A physical computer, not a VM instance (node).

host aggregate

A method to further subdivide availability zones into hypervisor pools, a collection of common hosts.

Host Bus Adapter (HBA)

Device plugged into a PCI slot, such as a fibre channel or network card.

hybrid cloud

A hybrid cloud is a composition of two or more clouds (private, community or public) that remain distinct entities but are bound together, offering the benefits of multiple deployment models. Hybrid cloud can also mean the ability to connect colocation, managed and/or dedicated services with cloud resources.

Hyper-V

One of the hypervisors supported by OpenStack.

hyperlink

Any kind of text that contains a link to some other site, commonly found in documents where clicking on a word or words opens up a different website.

Hypertext Transfer Protocol (HTTP)

An application protocol for distributed, collaborative, hypermedia information systems. It is the foundation of data communication for the World Wide Web. Hypertext is structured text that uses logical links (hyperlinks) between nodes containing text. HTTP is the protocol to exchange or transfer hypertext.

Hypertext Transfer Protocol Secure (HTTPS)

An encrypted communications protocol for secure communication over a computer network, with especially wide deployment on the Internet. Technically, it is not a protocol in and of itself; rather, it is the result of simply layering the Hypertext Transfer Protocol (HTTP) on top of the TLS or SSL protocol, thus adding the security capabilities of TLS or SSL to standard HTTP communications. most OpenStack API endpoints and many inter-component communications support HTTPS communication.

hypervisor

Software that arbitrates and controls VM access to the actual underlying hardware.

hypervisor pool

A collection of hypervisors grouped together through host aggregates.

IaaS

Infrastructure-as-a-Service. IaaS is a provisioning model in which an organization outsources physical components of a data center, such as storage, hardware, servers, and networking components. A service provider owns the equipment and is responsible for housing, operating and maintaining it. The client typically pays on a per-use basis. IaaS is a model for providing cloud services.

Icehouse

The code name for the ninth release of OpenStack. The design summit took place in Hong Kong and Ice House is a street in that city.

ICMP

Internet Control Message Protocol, used by network devices for control messages. For example, `ping` uses ICMP to test connectivity.

ID number

Unique numeric ID associated with each user in Identity, conceptually similar to a Linux or LDAP UID.

Identity API

Alternative term for the Identity service API.

Identity back end

The source used by Identity service to retrieve user information; an OpenLDAP server, for example.

identity provider

A directory service, which allows users to login with a user name and password. It is a typical source of authentication tokens.

Identity

The OpenStack core project that provides a central directory of users mapped to the OpenStack services they can access. It also registers endpoints for OpenStack services. It acts as a common authentication system. The project name of Identity is keystone.

Identity service API

The API used to access the OpenStack Identity service provided through keystone.

IDS

Intrusion Detection System.

image

A collection of files for a specific operating system (OS) that you use to create or rebuild a server. OpenStack provides pre-built images. You can also create custom images, or snapshots, from servers that you have launched. Custom images can be used for data backups or as "gold" images for additional servers.

Image API

The Image service API endpoint for management of VM images.

image cache

Used by Image service to obtain images on the local host rather than re-downloading them from the image server each time one is requested.

image ID

Combination of a URI and UUID used to access Image service VM images through the image API.

image membership

A list of tenants that can access a given VM image within Image service.

image owner

The tenant who owns an Image service virtual machine image.

image registry

A list of VM images that are available through Image service.

Image service

An OpenStack core project that provides discovery, registration, and delivery services for disk and server images. The project name of the Image service is glance.

Image service API

Alternative name for the glance image API.

image status

The current status of a VM image in Image service, not to be confused with the status of a running instance.

image store

The back-end store used by Image service to store VM images, options include Object Storage, local file system, S3, or HTTP.

image UUID

UUID used by Image service to uniquely identify each VM image.

incubated project

A community project may be elevated to this status and is then promoted to a core project.

ingress filtering

The process of filtering incoming network traffic. Supported by Compute.

INI

The OpenStack configuration files use an INI format to describe options and their values. It consists of sections and key value pairs.

injection

The process of putting a file into a virtual machine image before the instance is started.

instance

A running VM, or a VM in a known state such as suspended, that can be used like a hardware server.

instance ID

Alternative term for instance UUID.

instance state

The current state of a guest VM image.

instance tunnels network

A network segment used for instance traffic tunnels between compute nodes and the network node.

instance type

Describes the parameters of the various virtual machine images that are available to users; includes parameters such as CPU, storage, and memory. Alternative term for flavor.

instance type ID

Alternative term for a flavor ID.

instance UUID

Unique ID assigned to each guest VM instance.

interface

A physical or virtual device that provides connectivity to another device or medium.

interface ID

Unique ID for a Networking VIF or vNIC in the form of a UUID.

Internet protocol (IP)

Principal communications protocol in the internet protocol suite for relaying datagrams across network boundaries.

Internet Service Provider (ISP)

Any business that provides Internet access to individuals or businesses.

Internet Small Computer System Interface (iSCSI)

Storage protocol that encapsulates SCSI frames for transport over IP networks.

ironic

OpenStack project that provisions bare metal, as opposed to virtual, machines.

IOPS

IOPS (Input/Output Operations Per Second) are a common performance measurement used to benchmark computer storage devices like hard disk drives, solid state drives, and storage area networks.

IP address

Number that is unique to every computer system on the Internet. Two versions of the Internet Protocol (IP) are in use for addresses: IPv4 and IPv6.

IP Address Management (IPAM)

The process of automating IP address allocation, deallocation, and management. Currently provided by Compute, melange, and Networking.

IPL

Initial Program Loader.

IPMI

Intelligent Platform Management Interface. IPMI is a standardized computer system interface used by system administrators for out-of-band management of computer systems and monitoring of their operation. In layman's terms, it is a way to manage a computer using a direct network connection, whether it is turned on or not; connecting to the hardware rather than an operating system or login shell.

ip6tables

Tool used to set up, maintain, and inspect the tables of IPv6 packet filter rules in the Linux kernel. In OpenStack Compute, ip6tables is used along with arptables, ebtables, and iptables to create firewalls for both nodes and VMs.

ipset

Extension to iptables that allows creation of firewall rules that match entire "sets" of IP addresses simultaneously. These sets reside in indexed data structures to increase efficiency, particularly on systems with a large quantity of rules.

iptables

Used along with arptables and ebtables, iptables create firewalls in Compute. iptables are the tables provided by the Linux kernel firewall (implemented as different Netfilter modules) and the chains and rules it stores. Different kernel modules and programs are currently used for different protocols: iptables applies to IPv4, ip6tables to IPv6, arptables to ARP, and ebtables to Ethernet frames. Requires root privilege to manipulate.

IQN

iSCSI Qualified Name (IQN) is the format most commonly used for iSCSI names, which uniquely identify nodes in an iSCSI network. All IQNs follow the pattern iqn.yyyy-mm.domain:identifier, where 'yyyy-mm' is the year and month in which the domain was registered, 'domain' is the reversed domain name of the issuing organization, and 'identifier' is an optional string which makes each IQN under the same domain unique. For example, 'iqn.2015-10.org.openstack.408ae959bce1'.

iSCSI

The SCSI disk protocol tunneled within Ethernet, supported by Compute, Object Storage, and Image service.

ISO9660

One of the VM image disk formats supported by Image service.

itsec

A default role in the Compute RBAC system that can quarantine an instance in any project.

Java

A programming language that is used to create systems that involve more than one computer by way of a network.

JavaScript

A scripting language that is used to build web pages.

JavaScript Object Notation (JSON)

One of the supported response formats in OpenStack.

Jenkins

Tool used to run jobs automatically for OpenStack development.

jumbo frame

Feature in modern Ethernet networks that supports frames up to approximately 9000 bytes.

Juno

The code name for the tenth release of OpenStack. The design summit took place in Atlanta, Georgia, US and Juno is an unincorporated community in Georgia.

Kerberos

A network authentication protocol which works on the basis of tickets. Kerberos allows nodes communication over a non-secure network, and allows nodes to prove their identity to one another in a secure manner.

kernel-based VM (KVM)

An OpenStack-supported hypervisor. KVM is a full virtualization solution for Linux on x86 hardware containing virtualization extensions (Intel VT or AMD-V), ARM, IBM Power, and IBM zSeries. It consists of a loadable kernel module, that provides the core virtualization infrastructure and a processor specific module.

Key management service

OpenStack project that produces a secret storage and generation system capable of providing key management for services wishing to enable encryption features. The code name of the project is barbican.

keystone

The project that provides OpenStack Identity services.

Kickstart

A tool to automate system configuration and installation on Red Hat, Fedora, and CentOS-based Linux distributions.

Kilo

The code name for the eleventh release of OpenStack. The design summit took place in Paris, France. Due to delays in the name selection, the release was known only as K. Because k is the unit symbol for kilo and the reference artifact is stored near Paris in the Pavillon de Breteuil in Sèvres, the community chose Kilo as the release name.

large object

An object within Object Storage that is larger than 5 GB.

Launchpad

The collaboration site for OpenStack.

Layer-2 network

Term used in the OSI network architecture for the data link layer. The data link layer is responsible for media access control, flow control and detecting and possibly correcting errors that may occur in the physical layer.

Layer-3 network

Term used in the OSI network architecture for the network layer. The network layer is responsible for packet forwarding including routing from one node to another.

Layer-2 (L2) agent

OpenStack Networking agent that provides layer-2 connectivity for virtual networks.

Layer-3 (L3) agent

OpenStack Networking agent that provides layer-3 (routing) services for virtual networks.

Liberty

The code name for the twelfth release of OpenStack. The design summit took place in Vancouver, Canada and Liberty is the name of a village in the Canadian province of Saskatchewan.

libvirt

Virtualization API library used by OpenStack to interact with many of its supported hypervisors.

Lightweight Directory Access Protocol (LDAP)

An application protocol for accessing and maintaining distributed directory information services over an IP network.

Linux bridge

Software that enables multiple VMs to share a single physical NIC within Compute.

Linux Bridge neutron plug-in

Enables a Linux bridge to understand a Networking port, interface attachment, and other abstractions.

Linux containers (LXC)

An OpenStack-supported hypervisor.

live migration

The ability within Compute to move running virtual machine instances from one host to another with only a small service interruption during switchover.

load balancer

A load balancer is a logical device that belongs to a cloud account. It is used to distribute workloads between multiple back-end systems or services, based on the criteria defined as part of its configuration.

load balancing

The process of spreading client requests between two or more nodes to improve performance and availability.

LBaaS

Enables Networking to distribute incoming requests evenly between designated instances.

Logical Volume Manager (LVM)

Provides a method of allocating space on mass-storage devices that is more flexible than conventional partitioning schemes.

magnum

Code name for the OpenStack project that provides the Containers Service.

management API

Alternative term for an admin API.

management network

A network segment used for administration, not accessible to the public Internet.

manager

Logical groupings of related code, such as the Block Storage volume manager or network manager.

manifest

Used to track segments of a large object within Object Storage.

manifest object

A special Object Storage object that contains the manifest for a large object.

manila

OpenStack project that provides shared file systems as service to applications.

maximum transmission unit (MTU)

Maximum frame or packet size for a particular network medium. Typically 1500 bytes for Ethernet networks.

mechanism driver

A driver for the Modular Layer 2 (ML2) neutron plug-in that provides layer-2 connectivity for virtual instances. A single OpenStack installation can use multiple mechanism drivers.

melange

Project name for OpenStack Network Information Service. To be merged with Networking.

membership

The association between an Image service VM image and a tenant. Enables images to be shared with specified tenants.

membership list

A list of tenants that can access a given VM image within Image service.

memcached

A distributed memory object caching system that is used by Object Storage for caching.

memory overcommit

The ability to start new VM instances based on the actual memory usage of a host, as opposed to basing the decision on the amount of RAM each running instance thinks it has available. Also known as RAM overcommit.

message broker

The software package used to provide AMQP messaging capabilities within Compute. Default package is RabbitMQ.

message bus

The main virtual communication line used by all AMQP messages for inter-cloud communications within Compute.

message queue

Passes requests from clients to the appropriate workers and returns the output to the client after the job completes.

Message service

OpenStack project that aims to produce an OpenStack messaging service that affords a variety of distributed application patterns in an efficient, scalable and highly-available manner, and to create and maintain associated Python libraries and documentation. The code name for the project is zaqar.

Metadata agent

OpenStack Networking agent that provides metadata services for instances.

Meta-Data Server (MDS)

Stores CephFS metadata.

migration

The process of moving a VM instance from one host to another.

mistral

OpenStack project that provides the Workflow service.

Mitaka

The code name for the thirteenth release of OpenStack. The design summit took place in Tokyo, Japan. Mitaka is a city in Tokyo.

monasca

OpenStack project that provides a Monitoring service.

multi-host

High-availability mode for legacy (nova) networking. Each compute node handles NAT and DHCP and acts as a gateway for all of the VMs on it. A networking failure on one compute node doesn't affect VMs on other compute nodes.

multinic

Facility in Compute that allows each virtual machine instance to have more than one VIF connected to it.

murano

OpenStack project that provides an Application catalog.

Modular Layer 2 (ML2) neutron plug-in

Can concurrently use multiple layer-2 networking technologies, such as 802.1Q and VXLAN, in Networking.

Monitor (LBaaS)

LBaaS feature that provides availability monitoring using the `ping` command, TCP, and HTTP/HTTPS GET.

Monitor (Mon)

A Ceph component that communicates with external clients, checks data state and consistency, and performs quorum functions.

Monitoring

The OpenStack project that provides a multi-tenant, highly scalable, performant, fault-tolerant Monitoring-as-a-Service solution for metrics, complex event processing, and logging. It builds an extensible platform for advanced monitoring services that can be used by both operators and tenants to gain operational insight and visibility, ensuring availability and stability. The project name is monasca.

multi-factor authentication

Authentication method that uses two or more credentials, such as a password and a private key. Currently not supported in Identity.

MultiNic

Facility in Compute that enables a virtual machine instance to have more than one VIF connected to it.

network namespace

Linux kernel feature that provides independent virtual networking instances on a single host with separate routing tables and interfaces. Similar to virtual routing and forwarding (VRF) services on physical network equipment.

Nebula

Released as open source by NASA in 2010 and is the basis for Compute.

netadmin

One of the default roles in the Compute RBAC system. Enables the user to allocate publicly accessible IP addresses to instances and change firewall rules.

NetApp volume driver

Enables Compute to communicate with NetApp storage devices through the NetApp On-Command Provisioning Manager.

network

A virtual network that provides connectivity between entities. For example, a collection of virtual ports that share network connectivity. In Networking terminology, a network is always a layer-2 network.

NAT

Network Address Translation; Process of modifying IP address information while in transit. Supported by Compute and Networking.

network controller

A Compute daemon that orchestrates the network configuration of nodes, including IP addresses, VLANs, and bridging. Also manages routing for both public and private networks.

Network File System (NFS)

A method for making file systems available over the network. Supported by OpenStack.

network ID

Unique ID assigned to each network segment within Networking. Same as network UUID.

network manager

The Compute component that manages various network components, such as firewall rules, IP address allocation, and so on.

network node

Any compute node that runs the network worker daemon.

network segment

Represents a virtual, isolated OSI layer-2 subnet in Networking.

NTP

Network Time Protocol; Method of keeping a clock for a host or node correct via communication with a trusted, accurate time source.

network UUID

Unique ID for a Networking network segment.

network worker

The `nova-network` worker daemon; provides services such as giving an IP address to a booting nova instance.

Networking

A core OpenStack project that provides a network connectivity abstraction layer to OpenStack Compute. The project name of Networking is neutron.

Networking API

API used to access OpenStack Networking. Provides an extensible architecture to enable custom plug-in creation.

neutron

A core OpenStack project that provides a network connectivity abstraction layer to OpenStack Compute.

neutron API

An alternative name for Networking API.

neutron manager

Enables Compute and Networking integration, which enables Networking to perform network management for guest VMs.

neutron plug-in

Interface within Networking that enables organizations to create custom plug-ins for advanced features, such as QoS, ACLs, or IDS.

Nexenta volume driver

Provides support for NexentaStor devices in Compute.

No ACK

Disables server-side message acknowledgment in the Compute RabbitMQ. Increases performance but decreases reliability.

node

A VM instance that runs on a host.

non-durable exchange

Message exchange that is cleared when the service restarts. Its data is not written to persistent storage.

non-durable queue

Message queue that is cleared when the service restarts. Its data is not written to persistent storage.

non-persistent volume

Alternative term for an ephemeral volume.

north-south traffic

Network traffic between a user or client (north) and a server (south), or traffic into the cloud (south) and out of the cloud (north). See also east-west traffic.

nova

OpenStack project that provides compute services.

Nova API

Alternative term for the Compute API.

nova-network

A Compute component that manages IP address allocation, firewalls, and other network-related tasks. This is the legacy networking option and an alternative to Networking.

object

A BLOB of data held by Object Storage; can be in any format.

object auditor

Opens all objects for an object server and verifies the MD5 hash, size, and metadata for each object.

object expiration

A configurable option within Object Storage to automatically delete objects after a specified amount of time has passed or a certain date is reached.

object hash

Uniquely ID for an Object Storage object.

object path hash

Used by Object Storage to determine the location of an object in the ring. Maps objects to partitions.

object replicator

An Object Storage component that copies an object to remote partitions for fault tolerance.

object server

An Object Storage component that is responsible for managing objects.

Object Storage

The OpenStack core project that provides eventually consistent and redundant storage and retrieval of fixed digital content. The project name of OpenStack Object Storage is swift.

Object Storage API

API used to access OpenStack Object Storage.

Object Storage Device (OSD)

The Ceph storage daemon.

object versioning

Allows a user to set a flag on an Object Storage container so that all objects within the container are versioned.

Oldie

Term for an Object Storage process that runs for a long time. Can indicate a hung process.

Open Cloud Computing Interface (OCCI)

A standardized interface for managing compute, data, and network resources, currently unsupported in OpenStack.

Open Virtualization Format (OVF)

Standard for packaging VM images. Supported in OpenStack.

Open vSwitch

Open vSwitch is a production quality, multilayer virtual switch licensed under the open source Apache 2.0 license. It is designed to enable massive network automation through programmatic extension, while still supporting standard management interfaces and protocols (for example NetFlow, sFlow, SPAN, RSPAN, CLI, LACP, 802.1ag).

Open vSwitch (OVS) agent

Provides an interface to the underlying Open vSwitch service for the Networking plug-in.

Open vSwitch neutron plug-in

Provides support for Open vSwitch in Networking.

OpenLDAP

An open source LDAP server. Supported by both Compute and Identity.

OpenStack

OpenStack is a cloud operating system that controls large pools of compute, storage, and networking resources throughout a data center, all managed through a dashboard that gives administrators control while empowering their users to provision resources through a web interface. OpenStack is an open source project licensed under the Apache License 2.0.

OpenStack code name

Each OpenStack release has a code name. Code names ascend in alphabetical order: Austin, Bexar, Cactus, Diablo, Essex, Folsom, Grizzly, Havana, Icehouse, Juno, Kilo, Liberty, and Mitaka. Code names are cities or counties near where the corresponding OpenStack design summit took place. An exception, called the Waldon exception, is granted to elements of the state flag that sound especially cool. Code names are chosen by popular vote.

openSUSE

A Linux distribution that is compatible with OpenStack.

operator

The person responsible for planning and maintaining an OpenStack installation.

Orchestration

An integrated project that orchestrates multiple cloud applications for OpenStack. The project name of Orchestration is heat.

orphan

In the context of Object Storage, this is a process that is not terminated after an upgrade, restart, or reload of the service.

Oslo

OpenStack project that produces a set of Python libraries containing code shared by OpenStack projects.

parent cell

If a requested resource, such as CPU time, disk storage, or memory, is not available in the parent cell, the request is forwarded to associated child cells.

partition

A unit of storage within Object Storage used to store objects. It exists on top of devices and is replicated for fault tolerance.

partition index

Contains the locations of all Object Storage partitions within the ring.

partition shift value

Used by Object Storage to determine which partition data should reside on.

path MTU discovery (PMTUD)

Mechanism in IP networks to detect end-to-end MTU and adjust packet size accordingly.

pause

A VM state where no changes occur (no changes in memory, network communications stop, etc); the VM is frozen but not shut down.

PCI passthrough

Gives guest VMs exclusive access to a PCI device. Currently supported in OpenStack Havana and later releases.

persistent message

A message that is stored both in memory and on disk. The message is not lost after a failure or restart.

persistent volume

Changes to these types of disk volumes are saved.

personality file

A file used to customize a Compute instance. It can be used to inject SSH keys or a specific network configuration.

Platform-as-a-Service (PaaS)

Provides to the consumer the ability to deploy applications through a programming language or tools supported by the cloud platform provider. An example of Platform-as-a-Service is an Eclipse/Java programming platform provided with no downloads required.

plug-in

Software component providing the actual implementation for Networking APIs, or for Compute APIs, depending on the context.

policy service

Component of Identity that provides a rule management interface and a rule-based authorization engine.

pool

A logical set of devices, such as web servers, that you group together to receive and process traffic. The load balancing function chooses which member of the pool handles the new requests or connections received on the VIP address. Each VIP has one pool.

pool member

An application that runs on the back-end server in a load-balancing system.

port

A virtual network port within Networking; VIFs / vNICs are connected to a port.

port UUID

Unique ID for a Networking port.

preseed

A tool to automate system configuration and installation on Debian-based Linux distributions.

private image

An Image service VM image that is only available to specified tenants.

private IP address

An IP address used for management and administration, not available to the public Internet.

private network

The Network Controller provides virtual networks to enable compute servers to interact with each other and with the public network. All machines must have a public and private network interface. A private network interface can be a flat or VLAN network interface. A flat network interface is controlled by the flat_interface with flat managers. A VLAN network interface is controlled by the `vlan_interface` option with VLAN managers.

project

Projects represent the base unit of "ownership" in OpenStack, in that all resources in OpenStack should be owned by a specific project. In OpenStack Identity, a project must be owned by a specific domain.

project ID

User-defined alphanumeric string in Compute; the name of a project.

project VPN

Alternative term for a cloudpipe.

promiscuous mode

Causes the network interface to pass all traffic it receives to the host rather than passing only the frames addressed to it.

protected property

Generally, extra properties on an Image service image to which only cloud administrators have access. Limits which user roles can perform CRUD operations on that property. The cloud administrator can configure any image property as protected.

provider

An administrator who has access to all hosts and instances.

proxy node

A node that provides the Object Storage proxy service.

proxy server

Users of Object Storage interact with the service through the proxy server, which in turn looks up the location of the requested data within the ring and returns the results to the user.

public API

An API endpoint used for both service-to-service communication and end-user interactions.

public image

An Image service VM image that is available to all tenants.

public IP address

An IP address that is accessible to end-users.

public key authentication

Authentication method that uses keys rather than passwords.

public network

The Network Controller provides virtual networks to enable compute servers to interact with each other and with the public network. All machines must have a public and private network interface. The public network interface is controlled by the `public_interface` option.

Puppet

An operating system configuration-management tool supported by OpenStack.

Python

Programming language used extensively in OpenStack.

QEMU Copy On Write 2 (QCOW2)

One of the VM image disk formats supported by Image service.

Qpid

Message queue software supported by OpenStack; an alternative to RabbitMQ.

quarantine

If Object Storage finds objects, containers, or accounts that are corrupt, they are placed in this state, are not replicated, cannot be read by clients, and a correct copy is re-replicated.

Quick EMUlator (QEMU)

QEMU is a generic and open source machine emulator and virtualizer. One of the hypervisors supported by OpenStack, generally used for development purposes.

quota

In Compute and Block Storage, the ability to set resource limits on a per-project basis.

RabbitMQ

The default message queue software used by OpenStack.

Rackspace Cloud Files

Released as open source by Rackspace in 2010; the basis for Object Storage.

RADOS Block Device (RBD)

Ceph component that enables a Linux block device to be striped over multiple distributed data stores.

radvd

The router advertisement daemon, used by the Compute VLAN manager and FlatDHCP manager to provide routing services for VM instances.

rally

OpenStack project that provides the Benchmark service.

RAM filter

The Compute setting that enables or disables RAM overcommitment.

RAM overcommit

The ability to start new VM instances based on the actual memory usage of a host, as opposed to basing the decision on the amount of RAM each running instance thinks it has available. Also known as memory overcommit.

rate limit

Configurable option within Object Storage to limit database writes on a per-account and/or per-container basis.

raw

One of the VM image disk formats supported by Image service; an unstructured disk image.

rebalance

The process of distributing Object Storage partitions across all drives in the ring; used during initial ring creation and after ring reconfiguration.

reboot

Either a soft or hard reboot of a server. With a soft reboot, the operating system is signaled to restart, which enables a graceful shutdown of all processes. A hard reboot is the equivalent of power cycling the server. The virtualization platform should ensure that the reboot action has completed successfully, even in cases in which the underlying domain/VM is paused or halted/stopped.

rebuild

Removes all data on the server and replaces it with the specified image. Server ID and IP addresses remain the same.

Recon

An Object Storage component that collects meters.

record

Belongs to a particular domain and is used to specify information about the domain. There are several types of DNS records. Each record type contains particular information used to describe the purpose of that record. Examples include mail exchange (MX) records, which specify the mail server for a particular domain; and name server (NS) records, which specify the authoritative name servers for a domain.

record ID

A number within a database that is incremented each time a change is made. Used by Object Storage when replicating.

Red Hat Enterprise Linux (RHEL)

A Linux distribution that is compatible with OpenStack.

reference architecture

A recommended architecture for an OpenStack cloud.

region

A discrete OpenStack environment with dedicated API endpoints that typically shares only the Identity (keystone) with other regions.

registry

Alternative term for the Image service registry.

registry server

An Image service that provides VM image metadata information to clients.

Reliable, Autonomic Distributed Object Store

(RADOS)

A collection of components that provides object storage within Ceph. Similar to OpenStack Object Storage.

Remote Procedure Call (RPC)

The method used by the Compute RabbitMQ for intra-service communications.

replica

Provides data redundancy and fault tolerance by creating copies of Object Storage objects, accounts, and containers so that they are not lost when the underlying storage fails.

replica count

The number of replicas of the data in an Object Storage ring.

replication

The process of copying data to a separate physical device for fault tolerance and performance.

replicator

The Object Storage back-end process that creates and manages object replicas.

request ID

Unique ID assigned to each request sent to Compute.

rescue image

A special type of VM image that is booted when an instance is placed into rescue mode. Allows an administrator to mount the file systems for an instance to correct the problem.

resize

Converts an existing server to a different flavor, which scales the server up or down. The original server is saved to enable rollback if a problem occurs. All resizes must be tested and explicitly confirmed, at which time the original server is removed.

RESTful

A kind of web service API that uses REST, or Representational State Transfer. REST is the style of architecture for hypermedia systems that is used for the World Wide Web.

ring

An entity that maps Object Storage data to partitions. A separate ring exists for each service, such as account, object, and container.

ring builder

Builds and manages rings within Object Storage, assigns partitions to devices, and pushes the configuration to other storage nodes.

Role Based Access Control (RBAC)

Provides a predefined list of actions that the user can perform, such as start or stop VMs, reset passwords, and so on. Supported in both Identity and Compute and can be configured using the horizon dashboard.

role

A personality that a user assumes to perform a specific set of operations. A role includes a set of rights and privileges. A user assuming that role inherits those rights and privileges.

role ID

Alphanumeric ID assigned to each Identity service role.

rootwrap

A feature of Compute that allows the unprivileged "nova" user to run a specified list of commands as the Linux root user.

round-robin scheduler

Type of Compute scheduler that evenly distributes instances among available hosts.

router

A physical or virtual network device that passes network traffic between different networks.

routing key

The Compute direct exchanges, fanout exchanges, and topic exchanges use this key to determine how to process a message; processing varies depending on exchange type.

RPC driver

Modular system that allows the underlying message queue software of Compute to be changed. For example, from RabbitMQ to ZeroMQ or Qpid.

rsync

Used by Object Storage to push object replicas.

RXTX cap

Absolute limit on the amount of network traffic a Compute VM instance can send and receive.

RXTX quota

Soft limit on the amount of network traffic a Compute VM instance can send and receive.

S3

Object storage service by Amazon; similar in function to Object Storage, it can act as a back-end store for Image service VM images.

sahara

OpenStack project that provides a scalable data-processing stack and associated management interfaces.

SAML assertion

Contains information about a user as provided by the identity provider. It is an indication that a user has been authenticated.

scheduler manager

A Compute component that determines where VM instances should start. Uses modular design to support a variety of scheduler types.

scoped token

An Identity service API access token that is associated with a specific tenant.

scrubber

Checks for and deletes unused VMs; the component of Image service that implements delayed delete.

secret key

String of text known only by the user; used along with an access key to make requests to the Compute API.

secure shell (SSH)

Open source tool used to access remote hosts through an encrypted communications channel, SSH key injection is supported by Compute.

security group

A set of network traffic filtering rules that are applied to a Compute instance.

segmented object

An Object Storage large object that has been broken up into pieces. The re-assembled object is called a concatenated object.

self-service

For IaaS, ability for a regular (non-privileged) account to manage a virtual infrastructure component such as networks without involving an administrator.

SELinux

Linux kernel security module that provides the mechanism for supporting access control policies.

senlin

OpenStack project that provides a Clustering service.

server

Computer that provides explicit services to the client software running on that system, often managing a variety of computer operations. A server is a VM instance in the Compute system. Flavor and image are requisite elements when creating a server.

server image

Alternative term for a VM image.

server UUID

Unique ID assigned to each guest VM instance.

service

An OpenStack service, such as Compute, Object Storage, or Image service. Provides one or more endpoints through which users can access resources and perform operations.

service catalog

Alternative term for the Identity service catalog.

service ID

Unique ID assigned to each service that is available in the Identity service catalog.

service provider

A system that provides services to other system entities. In case of federated identity, OpenStack Identity is the service provider.

service registration

An Identity service feature that enables services, such as Compute, to automatically register with the catalog.

service tenant

Special tenant that contains all services that are listed in the catalog.

service token

An administrator-defined token used by Compute to communicate securely with the Identity service.

session back end

The method of storage used by horizon to track client sessions, such as local memory, cookies, a database, or memcached.

session persistence

A feature of the load-balancing service. It attempts to force subsequent connections to a service to be redirected to the same node as long as it is online.

session storage

A horizon component that stores and tracks client session information. Implemented through the Django sessions framework.

share

A remote, mountable file system in the context of the Shared File Systems. You can mount a share to, and access a share from, several hosts by several users at a time.

share network

An entity in the context of the Shared File Systems that encapsulates interaction with the Networking service. If the driver you selected runs in the mode requiring such kind of interaction, you need to specify the share network to create a share.

Shared File Systems API

A Shared File Systems service that provides a stable RESTful API. The service authenticates and routes requests throughout the Shared File Systems service. There is python-manilaclient to interact with the API.

Shared File Systems service

An OpenStack service that provides a set of services for management of shared file systems in a multi-tenant cloud environment. The service is similar to how OpenStack provides block-based storage management through the OpenStack Block Storage service project. With the Shared File Systems service, you can create a remote file system and mount the file system on your instances. You can also read and write data from your instances to and from your file system. The project name of the Shared File Systems service is manila.

shared IP address

An IP address that can be assigned to a VM instance within the shared IP group. Public IP addresses can be shared across multiple servers for use in various high-availability scenarios. When an IP address is shared to another server, the cloud network restrictions are modified to enable each server to listen to and respond on that IP address. You can optionally specify that the target server network configuration be modified. Shared IP addresses can be used with many standard heartbeat facilities, such as keepalive, that monitor for failure and manage IP failover.

shared IP group

A collection of servers that can share IPs with other members of the group. Any server in a group can share one or more public IPs with any other server in the group. With the exception of the first server in a shared IP group, servers must be launched into shared IP groups. A server may be a member of only one shared IP group.

shared storage

Block storage that is simultaneously accessible by multiple clients, for example, NFS.

Sheepdog

Distributed block storage system for QEMU, supported by OpenStack.

Simple Cloud Identity Management (SCIM)

Specification for managing identity in the cloud, currently unsupported by OpenStack.

Single-root I/O Virtualization (SR-IOV)

A specification that, when implemented by a physical PCIe device, enables it to appear as multiple separate PCIe devices. This enables multiple virtualized guests to share direct access to the physical device, offering improved performance over an equivalent virtual device. Currently supported in OpenStack Havana and later releases.

Service Level Agreement (SLA)

Contractual obligations that ensure the availability of a service.

SmokeStack

Runs automated tests against the core OpenStack API; written in Rails.

snapshot

A point-in-time copy of an OpenStack storage volume or image. Use storage volume snapshots to back up volumes. Use image snapshots to back up data, or as "gold" images for additional servers.

soft reboot

A controlled reboot where a VM instance is properly restarted through operating system commands.

Software Development Lifecycle Automation service

OpenStack project that aims to make cloud services easier to consume and integrate with application development process by automating the source-to-image process, and simplifying app-centric deployment. The project name is solum.

SolidFire Volume Driver

The Block Storage driver for the SolidFire iSCSI storage appliance.

solum

OpenStack project that provides a Software Development Lifecycle Automation service.

SPICE

The Simple Protocol for Independent Computing Environments (SPICE) provides remote desktop access to guest virtual machines. It is an alternative to VNC. SPICE is supported by OpenStack.

spread-first scheduler

The Compute VM scheduling algorithm that attempts to start a new VM on the host with the least amount of load.

SQL-Alchemy

An open source SQL toolkit for Python, used in OpenStack.

SQLite

A lightweight SQL database, used as the default persistent storage method in many OpenStack services.

stack

A set of OpenStack resources created and managed by the Orchestration service according to a given template (either an AWS CloudFormation template or a Heat Orchestration Template (HOT)).

StackTach

Community project that captures Compute AMQP communications; useful for debugging.

static IP address

Alternative term for a fixed IP address.

StaticWeb

WSGI middleware component of Object Storage that serves container data as a static web page.

storage back end

The method that a service uses for persistent storage, such as iSCSI, NFS, or local disk.

storage node

An Object Storage node that provides container services, account services, and object services; controls the account databases, container databases, and object storage.

storage manager

A XenAPI component that provides a pluggable interface to support a wide variety of persistent storage back ends.

storage manager back end

A persistent storage method supported by XenAPI, such as iSCSI or NFS.

storage services

Collective name for the Object Storage object services, container services, and account services.

strategy

Specifies the authentication source used by Image service or Identity. In the Database service, it refers to the extensions implemented for a data store.

subdomain

A domain within a parent domain. Subdomains cannot be registered. Subdomains enable you to delegate domains. Subdomains can themselves have subdomains, so third-level, fourth-level, fifth-level, and deeper levels of nesting are possible.

subnet

Logical subdivision of an IP network.

SUSE Linux Enterprise Server (SLES)

A Linux distribution that is compatible with OpenStack.

suspend

Alternative term for a paused VM instance.

swap

Disk-based virtual memory used by operating systems to provide more memory than is actually available on the system.

swawth

An authentication and authorization service for Object Storage, implemented through WSGI middleware; uses Object Storage itself as the persistent backing store.

swift

An OpenStack core project that provides object storage services.

swift All in One (SAIO)

Creates a full Object Storage development environment within a single VM.

swift middleware

Collective term for Object Storage components that provide additional functionality.

swift proxy server

Acts as the gatekeeper to Object Storage and is responsible for authenticating the user.

swift storage node

A node that runs Object Storage account, container, and object services.

sync point

Point in time since the last container and accounts database sync among nodes within Object Storage.

sysadmin

One of the default roles in the Compute RBAC system. Enables a user to add other users to a project, interact with VM images that are associated with the project, and start and stop VM instances.

system usage

A Compute component that, along with the notification system, collects meters and usage information. This information can be used for billing.

Telemetry

An integrated project that provides metering and measuring facilities for OpenStack. The project name of Telemetry is ceilometer.

TempAuth

An authentication facility within Object Storage that enables Object Storage itself to perform authentication and authorization. Frequently used in testing and development.

Tempest

Automated software test suite designed to run against the trunk of the OpenStack core project.

TempURL

An Object Storage middleware component that enables creation of URLs for temporary object access.

tenant

A group of users; used to isolate access to Compute resources. An alternative term for a project.

Tenant API

An API that is accessible to tenants.

tenant endpoint

An Identity service API endpoint that is associated with one or more tenants.

tenant ID

Unique ID assigned to each tenant within the Identity service. The project IDs map to the tenant IDs.

token

An alpha-numeric string of text used to access OpenStack APIs and resources.

token services

An Identity service component that manages and validates tokens after a user or tenant has been authenticated.

tombstone

Used to mark Object Storage objects that have been deleted; ensures that the object is not updated on another node after it has been deleted.

topic publisher

A process that is created when a RPC call is executed; used to push the message to the topic exchange.

Torpedo

Community project used to run automated tests against the OpenStack API.

transaction ID

Unique ID assigned to each Object Storage request; used for debugging and tracing.

transient

Alternative term for non-durable.

transient exchange

Alternative term for a non-durable exchange.

transient message

A message that is stored in memory and is lost after the server is restarted.

transient queue

Alternative term for a non-durable queue.

TripleO

OpenStack-on-OpenStack program. The code name for the OpenStack Deployment program.

trove

OpenStack project that provides database services to applications.

Ubuntu

A Debian-based Linux distribution.

unscoped token

Alternative term for an Identity service default token.

updater

Collective term for a group of Object Storage components that processes queued and failed updates for containers and objects.

user

In OpenStack Identity, entities represent individual API consumers and are owned by a specific domain. In OpenStack Compute, a user can be associated with roles, projects, or both.

user data

A blob of data that the user can specify when they launch an instance. The instance can access this data through the metadata service or config drive. Commonly used to pass a shell script that the instance runs on boot.

User Mode Linux (UML)

An OpenStack-supported hypervisor.

VIF UUID

Unique ID assigned to each Networking VIF.

VIP

The primary load balancing configuration object. Specifies the virtual IP address and port where client traffic is received. Also defines other details such as the load balancing method to be used, protocol, and so on. This entity is sometimes known in load-balancing products as a virtual server, vserver, or listener.

Virtual Central Processing Unit (vCPU)

Subdivides physical CPUs. Instances can then use those divisions.

Virtual Disk Image (VDI)

One of the VM image disk formats supported by Image service.

VXLAN

A network virtualization technology that attempts to reduce the scalability problems associated with large cloud computing deployments. It uses a VLAN-like encapsulation technique to encapsulate Ethernet frames within UDP packets.

Virtual Hard Disk (VHD)

One of the VM image disk formats supported by Image service.

virtual IP

An Internet Protocol (IP) address configured on the load balancer for use by clients connecting to a service that is load balanced. Incoming connections are distributed to back-end nodes based on the configuration of the load balancer.

virtual machine (VM)

An operating system instance that runs on top of a hypervisor. Multiple VMs can run at the same time on the same physical host.

virtual network

An L2 network segment within Networking.

virtual networking

A generic term for virtualization of network functions such as switching, routing, load balancing, and security using a combination of VMs and overlays on physical network infrastructure.

Virtual Network Computing (VNC)

Open source GUI and CLI tools used for remote console access to VMs. Supported by Compute.

Virtual Network InterFace (VIF)

An interface that is plugged into a port in a Networking network. Typically a virtual network interface belonging to a VM.

virtual port

Attachment point where a virtual interface connects to a virtual network.

virtual private network (VPN)

Provided by Compute in the form of cloudpipes, specialized instances that are used to create VPNs on a per-project basis.

virtual server

Alternative term for a VM or guest.

virtual switch (vSwitch)

Software that runs on a host or node and provides the features and functions of a hardware-based network switch.

virtual VLAN

Alternative term for a virtual network.

VirtualBox

An OpenStack-supported hypervisor.

VLAN manager

A Compute component that provides dnsmasq and radvd and sets up forwarding to and from cloudpipe instances.

VLAN network

The Network Controller provides virtual networks to enable compute servers to interact with each other and with the public network. All machines must have a public and private network interface. A VLAN network is a private network interface, which is controlled by the `vlan_interface` option with VLAN managers.

VM disk (VMDK)

One of the VM image disk formats supported by Image service.

VM image

Alternative term for an image.

VM Remote Control (VMRC)

Method to access VM instance consoles using a web browser. Supported by Compute.

VMware API

Supports interaction with VMware products in Compute.

VMware NSX Neutron plug-in

Provides support for VMware NSX in Neutron.

VNC proxy

A Compute component that provides users access to the consoles of their VM instances through VNC or VMRC.

volume

Disk-based data storage generally represented as an iSCSI target with a file system that supports extended attributes; can be persistent or ephemeral.

Volume API

Alternative name for the Block Storage API.

volume controller

A Block Storage component that oversees and coordinates storage volume actions.

volume driver

Alternative term for a volume plug-in.

volume ID

Unique ID applied to each storage volume under the Block Storage control.

volume manager

A Block Storage component that creates, attaches, and detaches persistent storage volumes.

volume node

A Block Storage node that runs the cinder-volume daemon.

volume plug-in

Provides support for new and specialized types of back-end storage for the Block Storage volume manager.

volume worker

A cinder component that interacts with back-end storage to manage the creation and deletion of volumes and the creation of compute volumes, provided by the cinder-volume daemon.

vSphere

An OpenStack-supported hypervisor.

weighting

A Compute process that determines the suitability of the VM instances for a job for a particular host. For example, not enough RAM on the host, too many CPUs on the host, and so on.

weight

Used by Object Storage devices to determine which storage devices are suitable for the job. Devices are weighted by size.

weighted cost

The sum of each cost used when deciding where to start a new VM instance in Compute.

worker

A daemon that listens to a queue and carries out tasks in response to messages. For example, the cinder-volume worker manages volume creation and deletion on storage arrays.

Workflow service

OpenStack project that provides a simple YAML-based language to write workflows, tasks and transition rules, and a service that allows to upload them, modify, run them at scale and in a highly available manner, manage and monitor workflow execution state and state of individual tasks. The code name of the project is mistral.

Xen

Xen is a hypervisor using a microkernel design, providing services that allow multiple computer operating systems to execute on the same computer hardware concurrently.

Xen API

The Xen administrative API, which is supported by Compute.

Xen Cloud Platform (XCP)

An OpenStack-supported hypervisor.

Xen Storage Manager Volume Driver

A Block Storage volume plug-in that enables communication with the Xen Storage Manager API.

XenServer

An OpenStack-supported hypervisor.

XFS

High-performance 64-bit file system created by Silicon Graphics. Excels in parallel I/O operations and data consistency.

zaqar

OpenStack project that provides a message service to applications.

ZeroMQ

Message queue software supported by OpenStack. An alternative to RabbitMQ. Also spelled 0MQ.

Zuul

Tool used in OpenStack development to ensure correctly ordered testing of changes in parallel.

www.ingramcontent.com/pod-product-compliance
Lightning Source LLC
LaVergne TN
LVHW060140070326
832902LV00018B/2881